CONTROLLING YOUR BRAND
IN THE AGE OF AMAZON

D1369846

CONTROLLING YOUR BRAND IN THE AGE OF AMAZON

The Brand Executive's Playbook For Winning Online

JAMES THOMSON AND WHITNEY GIBSON

LIBRARY OF CONGRESS CATALOGUING-IN-PUBLICATION DATA:
Thomson, James
Controlling Your Brand in the Age of Amazon:
The Brand Executive's Playbook For Winning Online /
James Thomson, Whitney Gibson.
p. cm.
ISBN 978-0-9984846-2-4 (paperback)
ISBN-978-0-9984846-3-1 (ebook Kindle)
1. Business 2. Law

Manufactured in the United States of America
First Edition

TABLE OF
CONTENTS

ACKNOWLEDGMENTS

WRITING THIS BOOK has been a team effort requiring the skills of many talented people.

We are fortunate to have hundreds of clients who have invited us into their organizations to test our ideas and then implement critical changes that we believe would better structure their organizations for long-term growth and profitability. Our clients remain unnamed, in deference to their confidentiality.

Our book-writing journey was made easier through the powerhouse editing of Jasmin Naim. We also thank Sara McKinniss, Emma Morehart and Rob Phillips—all from Vorys, Sater, Seymour and Pease LLP—for their advisory skills in turning our pile of papers into an informative book, from its infancy as a rough manuscript to the product it is today. If you want to challenge the ideas in the book, Whitney and James alone are responsible for any shortcomings.

This book has been improved through the discussions with and expert review of our trusted colleagues at Vorys, Sater, Seymour and Pease LLP, including: Daren Garcia, Colleen Devanney, Adam Sherman, Rajeev Adlakha, Rodney Holaday, T. Blake Finney, Timothy Ardizzone, Laura Erdman, Daniel Wucherer, Mark Zheng, Nina Webb-Lawton, Kenneth Rubin, Kara Mundy, Ted Mattis, and Jen House.

We thank Alexander Scott for his very sharp book cover design, and Spencer Durland for his animated video design. We also thank Phillip Gessert for designing the book layout. Together, they have enticed our readers to benefit fully from the content.

We thank the journalists who trusted us to share our perspectives in their coverage related to brand strategy and the Amazon marketplace. We also thank the hundreds of brand executives and Amazon sellers who shared their ideas and approaches on building their brands online and offline.

"I thank my Buy Box Experts business partner, Joseph Hansen, for his support and encouragement during the writing of this book. I thank Anne, Felix, Toby and Jasper, for their perpetual support during the never-ending rollercoaster ride as an entrepreneur. I also thank my parents Jeannette & Alan Thomson, and my friends Thomas Plaster, Clay Robinson, Steven Sperber, and Thang Nguyen, each for their unique skills in scrutinizing my ideas when we connect. My thanks to Jason Boyce and Jerry Kavesh for being my go-to buddies on all crazy Amazon developments. My thanks to Dipak Jain for encouraging me to develop expertise in an area where I could write a book and share my perspective. My special thanks to my wife Anne and my dear friends Bruce & Courtney Cameron for joining me in our journey learning about general merchandise reselling, exclusive reselling and product diversion."

—JAMES THOMSON, MERCER ISLAND, WASHINGTON

"First, I would like to thank my colleagues of Vorys eControl who have worked tirelessly to shape the practice to what it is today. I'd also like to thank my wife, Julie, and children, Emma, Avery and Charlie for their unwavering support. This has been a rewarding experience that I'm proud to be a part of."

—WHITNEY GIBSON, CINCINNATI, OHIO
FEBRUARY 2020

FOREWORD

In 2012, when Jeff Bezos said, "Your margin is my opportunity,"[1] he and the rest of the Amazon company had already been planning, operating, and fine-tuning the Amazon online marketplace for almost a decade. In 2005, Amazon launched its Prime program, and offered it to third-party sellers in 2006.[2] Amazon Prime fundamentally changed the way consumers buy products, both online and in brick-and-mortar stores. In 2012, Amazon's share of U.S. eCommerce sales was about 24%. In 2016, it was 33%. By 2018, it had jumped to 49%.[3] These numbers do not lie—Amazon's popularity took off, and many brands were not prepared.

Part of Amazon's success is that it runs open marketplaces, welcoming practically anyone to sell almost anything to Amazon customers. Amazon continues to add millions of third-party sellers to its Marketplaces[4] and

1. Lashinsky, A. (Nov. 16, 2012), *Amazon's Jeff Bezos: The Ultimate Disrupter*, FORTUNE, http://fortune.com/2012/11/16/amazons-jeff-bezos-the-ultimate-disrupter/ [Accessed January 18, 2020]
2. Weissmann, J. (March 13, 2014), *Amazon Is Jacking Up the Cost of Prime, and It's Still Cheap*, SLATE, https://slate.com/business/2014/03/amazon-prime-price-increase-its-still-inexpensive.html; Masters, K. (June 21, 2018), *Amazon Revolutionized Order Fulfillment, But This Company Is Creating Prime-Like Shipping For All*, FORBES, https://www.forbes.com/sites/kirimasters/2018/06/21/amazon-revolutionized-order-fulfillment-but-this-company-is-creating-prime-like-shipping-for-all/#74012a2a6a5a [Accessed January 18, 2020]
3. Molla, R. & Del Rey, J. (May 15, 2017), *Amazon's epic 20-year run as a public company, explained in five charts*, VOX, https://www.vox.com/2017/5/15/15610786/amazon-jeff-bezos-public-company-profit-revenue-explained-five-charts ; Lunden, I. (July 13, 2018), *Amazon's share of the US e-commerce market is now 49%, or 5% of all retail spend*, https://techcrunch.com/2018/07/13/amazons-share-of-the-us-e-commerce-market-is-now-49-or-5-of-all-retail-spend/ [Accessed January 18, 2020]
4. *Amazon Has 1,029,528 New Sellers This Year (Plus Other Stats)*, FEEDBACKEXPRESS.COM, https://www.feedbackexpress.com/amazon-1029528-new-sellers-year-plus-stats/ [Accessed January 18, 2020]

hundreds of millions of items to its catalog.[5] But many of these sellers are not authorized by the manufacturer of the products they sell, and offer diverted products to unwitting consumers enticed by Amazon's convenience, low price, and selection.

Brands of all sizes are feeling the impact of Amazon, especially if they are paying attention to their customers' buying patterns, either because the brand itself sells via Amazon or an unknown and unauthorized third-party seller sells the brand's products on Amazon—or both. This type of online sales structure on Amazon can disrupt a brand's established distribution strategy, creating channel conflict and frustration for both the brand and its authorized brick-and-mortar sellers. As a result, brands can no longer ignore the fact that their products will find a way onto the Amazon Marketplaces, and other online marketplaces, where someone can sell the products in ways that do not align with the brands' quality controls, customer service requirements, and other measures.

This book is for brand leaders who experience channel conflict and brand degradation and want to understand how to fix the problem, but do not know where to start. We pull back the curtains to reveal the combination of forces at play, as well as how the business and legal thinking of today's brand leaders must evolve for those brands to remain in control of their distribution and brand image.

Brand leaders need to adjust to the new environment that the online marketplaces have created. The following chapters are a playbook for brand leaders who are ready to protect their brands, motivated to sell their products, and incentivized to align their existing distribution strategy with the new eCommerce age.

James Thomson and Whitney Gibson
February 2020

---

5. (Jan. 15, 2018), *How Many Products Does amazon Sell Worldwide—January 2018*, SCRAPEHERO.COM, https://www.scrapehero.com/how-many-products-amazon-sell-worldwide-january-2018/ [Accessed January 18, 2020]

INTRODUCTION

INTRODUCTION

A brand for a company is like a reputation for a person. You earn reputation by trying to do hard things well.

—JEFF BEZOS

I MAGINE THAT YOU are an eCommerce executive for a large consumer packaged goods manufacturer. One sunny spring morning at work, the phone rings, and it is one of your largest retailers calling. It is clear from his tone that he is not happy. He says he cannot compete with the prices that your products are being advertised at on Amazon. His brick-and-mortar customers have stopped buying your products and now, he is stuck with inventory that he just cannot sell.

This is confusing to you; a couple of weeks ago, your director of sales assured you that none of your retailers were allowed to sell your products on online channels like Amazon. Yet, when you search for your brand on Amazon, it appears. Who are these sellers selling your products using ugly pictures with incomplete, incorrect product information? You have never heard of these sellers, and when you ask your director of sales, she has not heard of them either.

Or maybe the call you received was from the CEO of your company. She told you that, while she was at a business summit with other brand leaders, she was congratulated by a colleague for opening up product sales in Europe. Now, your CEO is asking you to confirm that the international expansion plans you both discussed last year were still shelved, and you were not quietly starting to work with European distributors. You are just as surprised as she is to discover that your products are for sale in Europe on one of the Amazon Marketplaces. You assure your CEO that you will look into it.

In both of these cases, you have at least three questions you need to answer:

1. How did this mess happen?
2. Who is responsible for this situation?
3. What can you do to fix it effectively?

If you are suffering from these types of issues today, you are hardly alone. In fact, in our professional experience, it is the exception and not the rule that large, popular brands have complete control of their online sales. But the brands that succeed both online and in brick-and-mortar channels are those that understand that the value of their brand depends on the investments they make in controlling product distribution today.

In the following chapters, we will address each of these issues:

- We examine how the retail environment has changed substantially with the rise of online marketplaces like Amazon.
- We explain what you—the senior brand, sales, legal or eCommerce executive—need to do to shift your company into the new world of brand stewardship.
- We will review some best practices used by leading brands today, and address the tough choices that executives will need to make if they are going to have any meaningful say in how their brands are represented to consumers online.

THE RETAIL ENVIRONMENT UNTIL 2000

TWO DECADES AGO, as a representative of your brand, you could decide when it was time to add new sales channels for your brand. You would organize your product catalogs and start calling on new retailers to carry your product. If you wanted to sell to Walmart or Bed, Bath, and Beyond, for example, you worked with a manufacturer representative or a consultant who could help get you in front of a buyer. You would make your pitch to the retailer's buyer, who would then decide whether to test out your product in that retail channel.

If you were fortunate enough to get the offer to sell into that retail channel, the retailer would place a purchase order with you, which you would fill out. You would have negotiated some terms with the retailer around merchandising, promotions, discounting, and possibly retail pricing. You also had a good idea of what was going to happen to your product once it was shipped to the retailer because:

- you knew the name of the retailer;
- it would be put on the shelf of the retailer;
- if you shipped 1,000 units to the retailer, then 1,000 units were made available for sale by the retailer on its shelves;
- if your products were sold in individual units, then 1,000 units were offered to consumers;
- if the arrangement was for the retailer to sell the product in U.S. stores, then the product was sold in U.S. stores; and
- if your product was shipped in consumer packaging that was, for example, blue with a specific Universal Product Code (UPC) your brand had acquired from GS1 (the organization that provides the standards for UPCs), then the product the consumer saw would be in the same blue consumer packaging with the same UPC.

Over time, as your products became more popular in those retail channels, you would continue to build a relationship with the retailer, discussing how to add new selections and otherwise modify inventory.

If you sold your products through a distributor, the distributor's job was to push your brand into new channels, and to negotiate on your behalf. The distributor would tell you when it had broken into a new retail channel, making both you and the distributor happy. There were a finite number of potential retailers for the distributor to pursue; this allowed the distributor to customize and focus its approach with each new retail channel.

The emergence of online marketplaces, like the Amazon Marketplace, suddenly brought both challenges and opportunities for brands, retailers, and distributors.

THE RETAIL ENVIRONMENT FROM 2000

IN 2000, AMAZON launched the Amazon Marketplace, welcoming third-party sellers to sell products alongside Amazon in its online channel. It would take at least five years before Amazon gained enough traction to have a diverse offering of product categories. While eBay had been operational as an auction site longer than Amazon's Marketplace, Amazon improved the customer experience through new technology and operational investments, including:

- buying A9.com, a product search technology company, in 2003;
- launching Amazon Prime, a two-day free delivery program, in 2005; and
- introducing Fulfillment By Amazon (FBA) to Amazon third-party sellers, making their products eligible for Amazon Prime as well, in 2006.

As Amazon added new features to the consumer shopping experience, the Marketplace grew in size—creating more customers, more sellers, and a much larger catalog of available products.

One of the key elements of the Marketplace was that Amazon allowed its online sellers to operate their stores under "Doing Business As" (DBA) names, making it easier for retailers to disguise their true identities. Importantly, Amazon did not—and does not—allow brands to decide who can sell their products.

As Amazon's Marketplace rose in popularity, something notable happened to players in the traditional retail space: consumers shifted purchasing decisions to online channels, opening up new types of choices—and eventually new challenges—for retailers, distributors, and brands.

RETAILERS could build sales on the Amazon channel, whether or not they had permission from brands, as the retailers could easily sell under DBA names. If retailers used the FBA program, even a brand regularly conducting test buys would struggle to determine the true identity of the Amazon seller. For a retailer looking to supplement its sales and profits with sales through this nascent online channel, it would be easy to recruit a plethora of sellers to join the Amazon Marketplace.

Retailers who were early adopters of the Amazon Marketplace channel often faced long periods of little to no competition in this online channel. Most retailers offset the sales commission fees that they paid Amazon with a reduction or elimination of the normal store overhead and staffing costs that brick-and-mortar channel sales created. However, as more sellers joined the Marketplace, competition increased and retailers found competitors driving down prices below what the retailers usually advertised in brick-and-mortar channels.

Amazon was systematic in its efforts to recruit not only more online sellers, but specifically retailers that had products and brands that were previously unavailable on Amazon. It also recruited more sellers of popular items already on the Marketplace, and this addition of specific listings led to competition as each retailer sought to beat the others for the sale. As Amazon increased product offerings on the Marketplace, more and more consumers started purchasing their favorite brands online. Amazon customers found products they wanted at prices they liked, and the products were delivered quickly to them, which created a pleasant shopping experience (especially if the products were shipped through FBA, making them Prime eligible).

DISTRIBUTORS quickly recognized two main advantages of the Amazon Marketplace channel:

1. they could become online retailers themselves, and
2. they could start supplying a new breed of online-only retailer that was capitalizing on the growth of this channel.

As online retailers themselves, the distributors had a cost advantage over any retailer to whom they might be wholesaling products. This cost advantage made the Amazon channel potentially very profitable if the distributor captured retail margins selling directly to consumers. Because the distributor could set up a DBA operation, it too could go undetected by a brand that did not want to be sold on Amazon. Often, distributors did not have to inform brands about how much volume they were selling to each retailer.

At the same time, online-only retailers started popping up looking for inventory to sell. They found distributors with products and purchased these products at wholesale prices. With little to none of the standard brick-and-mortar overhead, these online-only retailers made decent margins. If they used the FBA program for individual-order fulfillment, the online retailer might never have to handle any inventory and instead could ask the distributor to direct-ship products to Amazon's fulfillment centers. Distributors could capitalize on healthy volume discount programs that brands offered, so there was an incentive for distributors to buy more product than normal from the brand. They could divert excess to online retailers or their own third-party seller accounts on Amazon.

BRANDS also needed to adjust to the advent of the Amazon Marketplace. Successful brands recognized the unique opportunities the channel offered them: access to consumer data, opportunities to test out new products, and the possibilities of attractive margins (either wholesale margins on product sales to Amazon, or retail margins on product sales done through the brands' own third-party seller accounts). However, in the intervening period, most brands have not made the adjustments necessitated by the Amazon Marketplace, which is where we find ourselves today.

Most brands have not evolved. They have not adjusted their distribution strategies nor their work with retailers. They do not know how to survive in this new world of retail, one where 5 percent of product sales may be through the Amazon channel, but 80 percent of the brand's distribution challenges and questions surface from Amazon. To be clear: the Amazon channel is not so much the cause of the brand's distribution problem as it is where the brand's ineffective distribution efforts become apparent. We like to say that, AMAZON IS WHERE A BRAND'S DISTRIBUTION SINS SURFACE.

In today's world of retail, most brands:

- do not know the identity of their online resellers;
- do not know where these online resellers sourced inventory of the brand;
- do not know what proportion of inventory going through distributors is redirected to online channels;
- do not adequately police activities involving resellers that offer the brand's products in new multipack quantities defined by the reseller (rather than by the brand);

- cannot figure out how its brand is sold in countries where the brand does not yet have a distribution program of its own; and
- are not managing the branding, packaging and UPC labeling of online products adequately to ensure consistency between online and brick-and-mortar inventory.

What does it take for a brand to survive in this new environment? What controls need to be put in place? What existing sales and operational processes need to change? In the chapters that follow, we answer these questions.

Chapter 1 outlines the root of the problems brands face because of the rise of online marketplaces. In Chapter 2, we examine what strategy Amazon uses to pursue growth, and how this strategy complicates a company's brand control efforts. In Chapter 3, we look at product diversion forces outside Amazon that complicate brand control efforts. Starting with Chapter 4, we transition from addressing problems to discussing solutions. We begin in Chapter 4 by introducing the MARKETPLACE FLYWHEEL™ model that we have developed to show how a comprehensive brand governance strategy requires multiple, interconnected activities. Chapters 5 and 6 address specific actions brands can take to develop channel governance, while Chapter 7 examines catalog governance solutions and counterfeiting issues. In Chapter 8, we look at product diversion and brand control in the European market. Finally, in Chapter 9, we synthesize all of these concepts and urge brands to "sell upward."

Our book focuses on brands selling on marketplaces in the U.S. and the European Economic Area. As legal protections for brands differ around the world, we have chosen to focus on these specific markets where legal protections for brands are well established. For readers interested in applying brand control worldwide, we encourage them to seek legal guidance for each and every country where they plan to incorporate some form of distribution control and legal enforcement into their brand control efforts.

Throughout the book, we include some case studies of brands that have tackled these issues using a range of techniques, with varying levels of success and setback.

Let us begin tackling these challenges together.

WHAT IS THE PROBLEM?

CHAPTER 1

THE ROOT OF THE PROBLEM

You now have to decide what 'image' you want for your brand.
Image means personality. Products, like people, have
personalities, and they can make or break them in
the marketplace.

—DAVID OGILVY

ONLINE MARKETPLACES PROVIDE superior convenience, access to a vast array of products, and the ability to comparison shop with ease. These marketplaces are growing rapidly and are projected to keep growing at a dizzying rate. According to an Internet Retailer Study, shoppers in the United States made more than half of their eCommerce purchases on marketplaces in 2018.[1] And this is not just an American trend; marketplaces are also achieving massive growth internationally.

The online marketplace explosion has brought many new challenges for manufacturers and brands. Until recently, companies normally distributed their products as widely as possible without imposing any restrictions on where their products could be resold. That was not particularly troublesome before, but now the online marketplaces have created a new sales environment. For example, where there were barriers to entry to becoming an established retailer before, now there are few barriers to entry or exit and nearly anyone can sell products online. Additionally, now a customer who purchases a poor-quality product online from an

---

1. Fareeha, A. (March 13, 2019) *US ecommerce sales grow 15.0% in 2018*, DIGITAL COMMERCE 360, *https://www.digitalcommerce360.com/article/us-ecommerce-sales/* [Accessed January 18, 2020]

unauthorized seller can leave a negative review about the product online for consumers around the world to see. The confusing nature of the marketplaces also attributes to consumers' inability to know whether they are purchasing a product from the brand or from an unauthorized seller that does not abide by the brand's quality controls and customer service requirements.

Much of the difficulty in preserving brand value in the online marketplace era can be traced back to the traditional strategy employed by numerous consumer product companies, which favors wide, largely uncontrolled distribution. These companies hoped that their products would be sold freely in as many locations as possible. They may have sold to distributors (with whom the company may have had some type of agreement), who in turn sold to resellers (with whom the company likely had no agreement), who sold to anyone they chose, who may have sold yet again, and so on. Prior to the eCommerce explosion, the downsides of this model were not as readily visible or impactful.

With the omnipresence of powerful search engines and online marketplaces, virtually anyone can become a mini-distributor, retailer or instant international bargain-shopper. Downstream resellers or those who have acquired diverted products can simply open anonymous online marketplace storefronts at little-to-no cost and begin advertising products. Depending on their level in the supply chain, these unauthorized sellers may have access to significant product quantities, such that they are able to sell product in quantities that provide elevated placement in marketplace search engine results.

The retailers' heavily discounted advertised prices become immediately visible to all, and the proverbial race to the bottom ensues: all other resellers similarly scramble to drop their advertised prices, which harms the brand's positioning both in the market and in the minds of consumers. As the major online marketplaces deploy autonomous computer programs to compile pricing data on competitor websites (also known as scraping data), these resulting price drops can happen instantly. The end result is thwarted eCommerce sales growth, massive channel conflict and impaired brand value, which, left unchecked, will only get worse.

Legitimate distributors and resellers soon become angry when a company tries to charge them wholesale prices greater than the price at which products are advertised on online marketplaces. Indeed, many companies have experienced sales team meetings during which buyers from important retail customers negotiate by using their phones to identify and share multiple online listings for the same products at advertised prices significantly below the brand's wholesale price. Phone in hand, the retail customer simply demands lower wholesale prices. The company finds itself trapped and having to choose between protecting its brand value and its relationships with retailers, as more and more channel customers and consumers begin to compare products online before placing orders and making purchases.

As we will discuss in Chapters 5 and 6, unauthorized sellers also pay little heed to quality controls. Before the age of eCommerce, quality control issues may have been more tolerable because dissatisfied customers were unable to easily broadcast their dissatisfaction. However, in the age of eCommerce, customers who receive poor-quality products can effortlessly inform the whole world through negative product reviews. And customers—because they are not aware of the nature of the seller from whom they purchased—invariably blame the brand for quality issues rather than the seller.

These negative product reviews are highly influential, as online shoppers enjoy a plethora of choices and will typically rely on reviews to identify what they want. For instance, four out of five consumers have changed their minds about purchasing a product after reading negative reviews.[2] With smartphones ubiquitous, even customers who shop in brick-and-mortar outlets frequently refer to online reviews to assess the quality of the product they are thinking of purchasing.[3] Reviews also impact algorithms and search engine placement.[4] Thus, a cluster of negative reviews can be the death knell for a brand's sales even if they are caused by unauthorized sellers' lack of quality control.

Unauthorized sellers also free-ride on the promotional efforts of the brand and its authorized sellers. In a healthy distribution system, autho-

2. Kaemingk, D. (April 9, 2019) *20 online review states to know in 2019*, Qualtrics, https://www.qualtrics.com/blog/online-review-stats/ [Access January 18, 2020]

3. Skrovan, S. (June 7, 2017) *How shoppers use their smartphones in stores*, Retail Dive, *https://www.retaildive.com/news/how-shoppers-use-their-smartphones-in-stores/444147/* [Accessed January 18, 2020]

4. Baker, L. (Aug. 14, 2018) *Amazon's Search Engine Ranking Algorithm: What Marketers Need to Know*, Search Engine Journal, https://www.searchenginejournal.com/amazon-search-engine-ranking-algorithm-explained/265173/ [Accessed January 18, 2020]

rized sellers do not merely ship products to the consumer, but act as a brand's partners in promoting and marketing their products. Aside from benefits of these working arrangements, these activities impose certain burdens on authorized sellers, yet are critical for the long-term success of the brand. Unauthorized sellers do not take on these responsibilities, yet are in a position to capture sales from authorized sellers who do.

Companies today are struggling to adapt to this new environment of consumer confusion, negative online reviews, and influx of unauthorized sellers. How effectively companies can respond will determine whether they win or lose in this new reality. On one hand, some companies will fail to appropriately evolve to establish the heightened level of brand control now needed to succeed. These companies will likely experience channel conflict, degradation of brand value, and negative product reviews. Ultimately, they will be significantly handicapped in their efforts to protect and grow their brands.

On the other hand, there will be companies that realize the critical nature of retaking control of their online sales and will take the steps necessary to do so. These companies will be able to:

- maximize growth on existing and emerging online channels;
- execute viable minimum advertised price (MAP) programs where permissible;
- prevent channel conflict; and
- protect their brand value in the long term.

Like it or not, your brand's products will appear on online marketplaces. The question is whether your company can assert the control over your online sales necessary—particularly on marketplaces—to win in this dynamic market environment. In sum, because of the rise of online marketplaces, distribution choices for brands have changed. Most brands have not properly evolved their operations, marketing and sales incentives to capitalize on online marketplace opportunities while adequately protecting their brand equity. This book explains the process for doing so.

CHAPTER 2

DEMAND SIDE: THE AMAZON FLYWHEEL

The buyer is entitled to a bargain. The seller is entitled to a profit. So there is a fine margin in between where the price is right. I have found this to be true to this day whether dealing in paper hats, winter underwear or hotels.

—Conrad Hilton

WHY BRAND CONTROL IS CHALLENGING ON AMAZON

WHAT IS IT about the Amazon channel that has created so many brand control issues for manufacturers today? In this chapter, we examine what makes the Amazon channel unusually challenging for brands, as well as how brands often inadvertently contribute to these problems themselves.

AMAZON CHANNEL ISSUES CAUSING BRAND CONTROL CHALLENGES

UNFORTUNATELY, THE METHODS most brands use to protect brand equity have not evolved in concert with the growth of online marketplaces. Gone is the company's ability to decide when to enter new channels; instead, the brand will find its products being sold online by sellers who cannot be identified regardless of whether the brand wishes to be present there. Typically, these sellers acquire and resell the brand's products through product diversion, which is the practice of retailers selling product outside of channels authorized by the brand, often at a discount. While product diversion has been around for a long time in traditional retail channels,[1] the Amazon online channel offers several unique characteristics that make brand control ever more challenging.

Unlike most channels, Amazon has many features that directly or indirectly create channel control problems:

1. FEW BARRIERS TO ENTRY: With more than 1 million new third-party sellers joining Amazon in 2019,[2] the platform welcomes almost anyone to be a seller. There are few barriers to entry to signing up as an Amazon seller, and few limits on which brands an individual seller can offer.[3]

2. FEW BARRIERS TO EXIT: Amazon makes it easy for sellers to come and go from the platform, depending on inventory levels. Such low, fixed costs for sellers to maintain their status make it easier for them to show up with inventory from one-time buys, and get in and out of the channel as their inventory fluctuates.

3. SELLER DISPLAY NAMES: The Amazon.com and Amazon.ca (Canada) channels allow third-party sellers to operate under display names, which may be unrelated to their true name. If a brand cannot identify the Amazon seller by its display name, it is unlikely to know how to determine that seller's true identity. It is entirely possible, and likely, that many of these disguised sellers are retailers authorized by the brands to sell in other channels (but not Amazon).

4. AMAZON SCRAPING OUTSIDE PRICES: Amazon has developed web-scraping technology to compile product prices from thousands of websites, multiple times a day. In addition, it col-

---

1. AuthorizedStore.com (July 25, 2016) *Retailers jump on product diversion bandwagon*, https://www.authorizedstore.com/blog/index.php/2016/07/25/retailers-jump-on-product-diversion-bandwagon/ [Accessed January 18, 2020]

2. Marketplace Pulse, *Number of Sellers on Amazon Marketplace*, https://www.marketplacepulse.com/amazon/number-of-sellers [Accessed January 18, 2020]

3. Amazon Seller Central, *Selling Policies and Seller Code of Conduct*, https://sellercentral.amazon.com/gp/help/external/1801?language=en_US& ref=efph_1801_cont_521; *Sell on Amazon*, Amazon.com, https://services.amazon.com/content/ready-to-sell.html?ref_=asus_soa_gs_srcl_h [Accessed January 18, 2020]

lects offline pricing data. Through this effort, Amazon has a clear sense of the lowest prices for each Stock Keeping Unit (SKU), an alphanumeric code used for tracking and inventory purposes, across other shopping channels and in all its territories. Depending on how Amazon ranks the other shopping channel and the importance of a particular product to Amazon shoppers, it can update its own first-party prices within minutes. In other words, if Amazon were to see a particular product priced lower on Walmart.com or another retailer's website, for example, Amazon would likely price-match quickly because these channels are retail rivals of significant scale. Not only that, if a brand were to run a regional pricing special in one part of the country, Amazon's price scrapers would most likely find that special, providing Amazon with the data needed to match it. In either case, Amazon's ability to collect and act on pricing data across the country quickly gives it the ability to ensure that it is at or very near the lowest prices for key products and to do so in a targeted way. These actions suggest that Amazon views competitively low prices as critical to the Amazon customer experience.[4][5]

5. AMAZON IS NOT INVOLVED IN ENFORCING DISTRIBUTION AGREEMENTS: Amazon has made it clear that it will not participate in helping brands to identify unauthorized sellers, nor will it remove them from its Marketplace. In Sellercentral.amazon.com (the portal that third-party sellers use with Amazon), Amazon states:

> *Exclusive or Selective Distribution: Amazon respects a manufacturer's right to enter into exclusive distribution agreements for its products. However, violations of such agreements do not constitute intellectual property rights*

4. Hanbury, M. (Nov. 9, 2018) *Amazon is triggering a battle for rock-bottom prices*, Business Insider, https://www.businessinsider.com/amazon-has-cheapest-prices-study-says-2018-11 [Accessed January 18, 2020]

5. Loeb, W. (Nov. 20, 2014) *Amazon's Pricing Strategy Makes Life Miserable For The Competition*, Forbes, https://www.forbes.com/sites/walterloeb/2014/11/20/amazons-pricing-strategy-makes-life-miserable-for-the-competition/#e2252595c609 [Accessed January 18, 2020]

infringement. As the enforcement of these agreements is a matter between the manufacturer and the retailers, it would not be appropriate for Amazon to assist in enforcement activities.[6]

It is worth noting that Amazon's mode of operation includes actively recruiting multiple sellers on the same listings. Listing multiple sellers increases the likelihood of intrabrand price competition, which results in happier customers. The more competition and the lower the prices that Amazon can generate on its platform, the more likely customers are to return to the channel.

6. A BRAND HAS LITTLE SAY REGARDING ITS PRESENCE ON THE CHANNEL: The Amazon channel allows products to be offered for sale even when the brand has no interest in seeing its products sold there and has never authorized the same.

7. AMAZON 1P PURCHASES DIVERTED PRODUCTS: Not only does Amazon serve as a platform for third-party sellers who offer diverted products to Amazon customers, but Amazon's own Vendor Management/First-Party (1P) operation also purchases products from sources that a brand may not have authorized to wholesale its products to Amazon. Distributors and resellers have been able to create Vendor Central accounts where they can offer products for Amazon to wholesale from them. This shows that Amazon will purchase products from resellers that offer the lowest wholesale prices, resulting in situations where the brand company is competing with its own distributors (often unknowingly) selling wholesale products to Amazon 1P. If Amazon is able to buy the products wholesale from a distributor or reseller at a lower price than from the brand company itself, it will do so.

Buy Box Experts has encountered client situations where the brand company did not realize Amazon was buying the brand's products from sources other than the brand company itself, and

---

6. Amazon Seller Central, *Intellectual property for Rights Owner,* *https://sellercentral.amazon.com/gp/help/GU5SQCEKADDAQRLZ* [Accessed January 18, 2020]

was able to show them, by monitoring the SKUs, that Amazon 1P was retailing different products from those offered to Amazon by the brand company.

8. AMAZON 1P MOVES INVENTORY ACROSS BORDERS: Amazon 1P often moves inventory across borders to make products available in its other geographic Marketplaces. This can come as a surprise to a brand that thought it was doing business only with Amazon's U.S. operations. Essentially, Amazon 1P may be influencing a brand's overseas distribution strategy, without the brand realizing this until it is too late. Buy Box Experts has worked with brands that have tried to stop Amazon 1P from moving their products across borders, and found themselves unable to do so.

9. THE AMAZON 3P PLATFORM FACILITATES 3P SELLERS SELLING ACROSS BORDERS: Regardless of whether a 3P seller is authorized or not by the brand to sell in a given geographic Marketplace, Amazon continues to roll out its cross-border shipping options for 3P sellers, making it much easier for Amazon customers in one country to buy products from sellers in other Amazon Marketplaces where prices might be lower and availability higher. Cross-border shipping by Amazon could result in an authorized American 3P seller inadvertently selling through the Amazon EU Marketplaces, for example, even though the brand may not want the 3P seller to do so. Such unauthorized cross-border shipping into other marketplaces could have negative consequences for the brand. As a hypothetical, imagine that a brand sells children's toys with small parts and labels the products intended for sale in another country differently than those in the U.S. It does so because the other country imposes different requirements on warning labels for products that could be a choking hazard for children. The inadvertent sale of a U.S. product in the other country that does not comply with the labeling requirements could cause serious problems for the brand, despite its efforts to label products differently and control its sales channels.

10. CUSTOMER IGNORANCE OF THE RELATIVE AGE OF PRODUCTS: Customers do not usually know which model of a

brand's product is the most recent. 3P sellers use this to their advantage, capitalizing on brands' year-end closeouts or liquidations, in order to procure product at much lower costs. They can then resell the older product versions on Amazon for high margins to customers who do not realize that they are not buying the current product model. While the brand may think in terms of this year's and last year's models, low prices on last year's models can drive up sales and organic search results generally on the brand's products on Amazon. The brand's efforts to clear out old inventory will actually help product diverters or unauthorized sellers to dominate the sales activity of the brand on the Amazon channel by providing them a source of low-cost inventory and driving increased traffic for all of the brand's products on Amazon.

11. FBA COMMINGLING: Third-party sellers using Amazon's FBA program may choose to use a feature Amazon calls commingling, through which Amazon blends the physical inventories of multiple sellers, making it nearly impossible to identify which seller supplied which units of inventory. This practice prevents a brand from being able to ensure its products purchased on Amazon have been subject to its quality controls and are of the high quality consumers expect of the brand.

12. LOST FBA INVENTORY IS A SOURCE OF DIVERTED PRODUCT: If a seller ships FBA inventory to Amazon but Amazon misplaces it, Amazon will reimburse the seller for that inventory. This means that if Amazon later finds the inventory, Amazon owns it and can resell it. Amazon may choose to sell that newly found inventory under its Amazon Warehouse Deals seller account, or it may batch up this inventory with other lost FBA inventory, and sell it in pallets to the highest bidder. In turn, that highest bidder may choose to sell it on Amazon or elsewhere, without the brand's explicit permission or knowledge.

13. IRRATIONAL PRICING BY SOME 3P SELLERS: Sadly, it is easy to be a 3P seller on Amazon without a clear understanding of unit economics. Many sellers will look at the aggregate top and bottom-line sales numbers, without the sophistication of breaking

out costs by SKU. As a result, some products will be unknowingly sold below cost, resulting in competitive forces that authorized sellers (and brands) cannot rationalize or compete with.

14. SEARCH COSTS OF PRICES ON THE AMAZON CHANNEL: Recent studies indicate that nearly 54 percent of in-store American consumers use their smartphones to do price comparisons.[7] Anyone with a phone in his/her hand can check retail prices on Amazon instantaneously from anywhere. This availability of the data makes it easier for consumers to walk into a brick-and-mortar store, look at a product, but decide to purchase it instead on Amazon. Likewise, a current or potential distributor or retailer can cross-reference prices on Amazon to see if the wholesale prices proposed by the brand or a distributor make any profitable or competitive sense. If not, the distributor or retailer may decide to walk away from sourcing products.

15. PRIME ELIGIBILITY: Amazon offers sellers access to Prime eligibility through the FBA program, reducing customers' focus on the identity of the actual seller and increasing sellers' ability to remain anonymous and function without authority from a brand.

16. PRODUCT PROVENANCE IS NOT USUALLY IMPORTANT: Amazon does not (and is not obligated to) question the source of products being sold on its Marketplace, as long as they are not counterfeit.[8] Although Amazon's policies generally prohibit sellers from acting in a way that infringes another's intellectual property rights, Amazon does not conduct pre-sale review of all products on its Marketplace.[9]

7. Skrovan, S. (June 7, 2017) *How shoppers use their smartphones in stores*, Retail Dive, *https://www.retaildive.com/news/how-shoppers-use-their-smartphones-in-stores/444147/* [Accessed January 18, 2020]
8. Amazon Seller Central, *Amazon Anti-Counterfeiting Policy*, https://sellercentral.amazon.com/gp/help/external/201165970 [Accessed January 18, 2020]
9. Amazon Seller Central, *Intellectual property for Rights Owners*, https://sellercentral.amazon.com/gp/help/external/help.html?itemID=U5SQCEKADDAQRLZ&ref=efph_U5SQCEKADDAQRLZ_cont_G2 [Accessed January 18, 2020]

17. SINGLE-LISTING MODEL: Amazon combines multiple offers for the same product into a single listing without conspicuously identifying the seller for each offer. This model makes it difficult for sellers to compete on anything other than price and creates a more confusing customer experience by presenting the offers across all sellers on a single listing, making it difficult for consumers to know who the seller is, rather than using separate product listings for each seller.

18. INTRA-LISTING COMPETITION REDUCES SEARCH COSTS: Amazon has helped to reduce information search costs, as consumers can instantly determine the prices of various sellers' offers on one site, rather than having to call different retail stores or walking through physical stores to do comparison shopping on pricing and selection availability.

19. RANKING DEMAND: Amazon reveals the sales rank of individual products in their categories, making it easier for additional prospective sellers to pinpoint which products have the highest demand.

20. 1P'S DESTABILIZING EFFECTS ON PRICING: Unlike most other marketplaces, Amazon ensures its continuing relevance and success by procuring through its 1P program top-selling products from direct and indirect channels and using its web-scraping technology to collect pricing data and usually offer the lowest price of all other marketplaces and all other sellers on its own Marketplace.

21. AMAZON'S PLACEMENT ON SEARCH ENGINES: Search engines like Google use algorithms to index Amazon content much higher than most other online sites. As a result, the product listing of a new brand on Amazon is likely to be indexed higher on Google, even if the brand is not yet sold in large quantities across Amazon. With higher Amazon organic search results on search engines, Amazon's product listings are more visible to search engine consumers, driving more customers back to shop on Amazon.

22. AMAZON'S SUPPRESSION OF THE BUY BOX: The "add to cart" button a consumer clicks to purchase a product is called the buy box, and Amazon uses an algorithm to determine which seller's

product lands the buy box. Amazon can also alter a product detail page so that the buy box does not appear, called supressing the buy box. Amazon may do this for several reasons, including if the sellers' sales volumes are too low or Amazon believes the lowest price offered is too high.[10]

23. INERTIA OF THE AMAZON MARKETPLACE: With 105 million U.S. Prime customers (and many more non-Prime customers) recorded by mid-2019,[11] the sheer volume of search and purchase activity is so large that the channel's impact on setting consumers' price expectations can hardly be matched by other retail channels.

Case Study: Brand loses buy box eligibility for all its Amazon listings, due to a lack of Amazon control combined with a switch from 1P to 3P

BUSINESS CHALLENGE: A mid-sized toy brand had recently pivoted from 1P to 3P, changing its distribution model in an effort to mitigate the retail price discounting instigated by Amazon 1P and help protect its brand value. The brand had established that Amazon 1P was matching prices on other online marketplaces, where companies were selling the brand's products at prices far lower than the brand's preferred prices. Unfortunately, shortly after becoming a 3P seller, the brand found that Amazon suppressed the buy box on all of its Amazon listings, making it no longer possible for any other seller to win the buy box. With this suppression came a steep drop in overall sales across the Amazon channel. Because Amazon actively scrapes competitor websites for prices of brands that are carried on Amazon (both 1P and key 3P brands), inevitably it

---

10. Maplesden, P. *How to Win The Amazon Buy Box: Your Questions Answered*, https://www.webretailer.com/b/amazon-buy-box/#What_is_Buy_Box_suppression [Accessed January 18, 2020]

11. Clement, J., *Number of Amazon Prime members in the United States as of June 2019 (in millions)*, Statista.com, *http://fortune.com/2017/10/18/amazon-prime-customer-spending/* [Accessed January 18, 2020]

found that prices for the brand's listings on the other marketplaces continued to be cheaper than on Amazon.

SOLVING THE ISSUE: Solving the Amazon buy box problem required first solving the overall channel conflict problem. So the brand made the tough decision to cut off all companies that it knew were selling products on the other marketplaces. After a couple of months, once inventory of these sellers dried up, there was no longer an active price against which Amazon could benchmark its prices of the brand's products.

RESOLUTION: While suppression of the buy box on Amazon was lifted for some products, the brand was not completely able to eliminate all sellers selling below the manufacturer suggested retail price (MSRP) in the many other online channels monitored by Amazon. So, the brand decided to continue selling a limited selection of products through Amazon 1P—specifically, SKUs where the brand continued to have distribution control issues. For these products, Amazon 1P immediately went back to winning the buy box. On those parts of its catalog where the brand did not face retail pricing discrepancies brought on by unauthorized price discounting by other sellers, the brand sold those items through its 3P account, recapturing its buy-box-winning position.

What was particularly frustrating for the brand about this process was seeing Amazon 1P winning the buy box at prices 10-15 percent higher than the prices that continued to exist on the other marketplaces. Amazon 1P was apparently willing to give itself the buy box if it had supply, but would suppress the buy box altogether if it did not remain able to buy the products from the brand.

With a basic understanding of Amazon's key features, let us review the strategy that Amazon uses to drive its Marketplace growth. For nearly two decades, Amazon has focused its efforts to grow around a number of key choices that it has made.

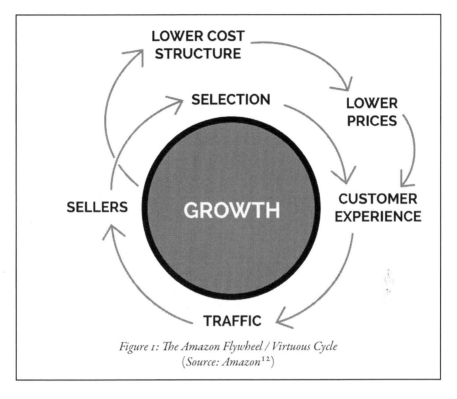

Figure 1: The Amazon Flywheel / Virtuous Cycle
(Source: Amazon[12])

In his 2013 book, *The Everything Store*, New York Times-bestselling author Brad Stone wrote that:

> *Bezos and his lieutenants sketched their own virtuous cycle, which they believed powered their business. It went something like this: lower prices led to more customer visits. More customers increased the volume of sales and attracted more commission-paying third-party sellers to the site. That allowed Amazon to get more out of fixed costs like the fulfillment centers and the servers needed to run the website. This greater efficiency then enabled it to lower prices further. Feed any part of this flywheel, they reasoned, and it should accelerate the loop.[13]*

12. *About Amazon*, https://www.amazon.jobs/en/landing_pages/about-amazon [Accessed January 18, 2020]
13. Stone, B. (2013) *The Everything Store: Jeff Bezos and the Age of Amazon*, London, Bantam Press

From a brand's perspective, there are several key implications of this virtuous cycle on how a brand can control its online sales:

1. Amazon is more interested in lower prices than higher margins, so we can expect lower prices to emerge on the channel.
2. Amazon seeks to add more sellers to compete against one another, again driving deeper intrabrand competition.
3. Brands, per se, are not part of the virtuous cycle—yes, a brand's individual products are part of selection (see Figure 1), but the Amazon channel is not meant to be a curated shopping destination the way a high-end shopping mall might be selective about which brands are recruited to participate. Amazon focuses on whether a brand is in demand by its customers more than whether the brand is a high-end, mid-level or low-end brand. Regardless of price, if a particular brand is in high demand on Amazon, there is likely a plan in place to find additional sellers who will add more selection (and hence intrabrand competition) into the overall Amazon catalog.
4. A seller is recruited to the platform without too many questions about the provenance of the seller's inventory.
5. The focal customer in this model is the end consumer, not the brand or the seller.

Given the massive, ever-growing size of the Amazon channel, more U.S. customers each day start their product search online on Amazon than any other online channel in the U.S.[14]

Case Study: Brand dealing with lack of channel control overhauls its distribution strategy

BUSINESS CHALLENGE: When Amazon 1P approached a specialty food company, the brand was excited about the prospect of

---

14. *The Competitive State of eCommerce Marketplaces: Data Report Q2 2018* (2018) Jumpshot, Inc., *http://go.jumpshot.com/rs/677-KZC-213/images/Jumpshot-Q2-Data-Report.pdf* [Accessed January 18, 2020]

significant increases in online sales. Amazon 1P placed a large initial purchase order, which was happily filled by the brand. While Amazon continued to place multiple purchase orders, within six months they hit a wall—Amazon 1P was selling the product to Amazon customers at prices nearly equivalent to the brand's wholesale price, and the brand did not know what to do. Amazon 1P bought pallets of large-quantity multipacks from the brand, then broke them down to sell as individual unit products on Amazon.com. As a result of the heavy discounts that came with the large-quantity multipacks, Amazon still made margin selling these smaller unit products.

At the same time, the brand was actively seeking new distributors as well as brick-and-mortar retailers to carry its products in their stores. With Amazon's pricing publicly visible, the brand encountered huge problems attracting interest from retailers asked to pay wholesale prices that were almost the same as the retail prices that Amazon had created for itself through unbundling. After less than a year of engaging with Amazon, the brand's largest retailer dropped the brand completely, saying it made no financial sense to continue the relationship. This loss resulted in an immediate 20 percent drop in the brand's revenue.

SOLVING THE ISSUE: With a situation complex enough to confound most executives, the brand announced to Amazon 1P that it was immediately cutting off supply of all product. Next, the brand opened up a 3P account, much to Amazon's displeasure. The Vendor Management team at Amazon threatened that if the brand left 1P, it would never be welcomed back to 1P (an empty threat, as the brand had no interest in ever returning to 1P). The brand leadership knew it had to make this critical change, or likely lose all distribution partners in other channels.

RESOLUTION: With 1P running out of inventory within a few weeks and no longer able to be replenished, the brand saw its 3P business slowly grow. More importantly, retail prices across channels stabilized quickly, because Amazon 1P was no longer driving down the retail prices that were used as a baseline by all the other channels where the brand was retailed.

Within the next 24 months, the brand grew its off-Amazon channel sales by more than 200 percent, and was able to continue to build a modest 3P business. Having initially thought that adding the Amazon channel would be a big lift overall, the brand's inability to control how Amazon 1P broke down multipacks and reduced advertised pricing nearly killed it. In the end, the brand took back control of its distribution, and with that, the ability to protect its brand equity across all channels.

BRAND-DRIVEN ISSUES CAUSING BRAND CONTROL CHALLENGES

PUT BLUNTLY, MOST brands have all sorts of distribution leaks that are being leveraged to supply product via online marketplace channels like Amazon. We examine how product diversion is created by the combination of:

- distribution channels that are being inadequately managed by brands, with
- opportunistic intermediaries and retailers who see a chance to make money.

As discussed, PRODUCT DIVERSION is the practice of unauthorized retailers or distributors selling product outside of channels authorized by the brand, often at prices lower than the brand's preferred retail price points. As Amazon has grown into an online marketplace with more than 500 million product listings and more than 3 million sellers supplying those products, any brand with decent consumer awareness or popularity should expect that someone has found a way to offer their products on the Amazon Marketplace with or without the brand's permission. With the establishment and unprecedented growth of large, online marketplaces like Amazon, product diversion has flourished, and many brand executives are feeling helpless to prevent this practice from spreading.

The problem of product diversion has in truth always existed, however the Amazon Marketplace has exacerbated it. The traffic and sales volume captured by Amazon not only increase the visibility of an existing product diversion problem, but also accelerate its growth[15] (now that there is enough demand on Amazon to motivate distributors and retailers to participate in either diverting product, or selling grey market products).

In summary, the open, opportunistic nature of Amazon, which allows practically anyone to sell on its Marketplace, impacts brands in ways previously unfamiliar to most of them. If a brand has not adequately controlled the distribution of its products across all offline and online channels, unknown online sellers can quickly erode the brand's value and ability to message consistent brand promises across all channels and in all territories.

---

15. *Retailers jump on product diversion bandwagon* (July 25, 2016) authorizedstore.com, https://www.authorizedstore.com/blog/index.php/2016/07/25/retailers-jump-on-product-diversion-bandwagon/ [Accessed January 18, 2020]

CHAPTER 3

SUPPLY SIDE: DIVERSION

I don't design down to a price.

—James Dyson

WHY PRODUCT DIVERSION SHOULD MATTER TO YOUR BRAND

AT A FUNDAMENTAL level, a branded product is an item in which significant investments have been made to secure the consistent delivery of features and benefits to customers. Due to the way the company has positioned, protected and marketed the brand, those customers have come to understand these features and benefits and associate them with the brand. As the brand builds out its distribution channels to access more groups of customers, it becomes more challenging to maintain consistency around brand messaging and perceived brand value.

Product diversion creates numerous challenges for brands, including:

1. Online advertised pricing is usually lower than advertised pricing anywhere else. When customers learn that they can find lower prices on one channel, they typically neglect other channels. And so the brand ends up with brick-and-mortar retailers (and their distributors) complaining that they cannot compete with unmanaged online channels.
2. When there is conflict between online and offline channels, it does not take long before distributors find it harder to recruit new brick-and-mortar retailers to carry the brand. And if the conflict becomes large enough, the distributor will see its wholesale pricing at levels barely lower than the unauthorized

online resellers' prices. At this point, quality channel customers cannot make a sufficient margin. The distributor then either declines to carry the brand, or forces a renegotiation of wholesale pricing.

3. For every unauthorized online reseller who advertises product below minimum advertised price (MAP) or manufacturer suggested retail price (MSRP), there are a number of high quality authorized resellers who are trying hard to follow the brand's pricing policies, but are finding they cannot achieve a sufficient level of sales. Because the brand often does not know how to eliminate unauthorized seller activity, authorized retailers naturally feel more motivated to reduce prices.

4. When unauthorized sellers show up online, they have often created their own product listings. This means that they use content that does not offer the complete, accurate and consistent messages that the brand has heavily invested in developing and distributing throughout its managed channels.

5. Customer confusion surfaces when diverted product shows up online. Online shoppers may feel they are getting a good deal, but do not know at what cost. Is the product authentic? Is it new? Is it damaged or different in some way compared with what the shopper might get from a clearly authorized reseller? Unfortunately, some product categories, such as apparel and beauty products, are also plagued with counterfeit products, where a high consumer demand and a lack of distribution control make it easier to mingle counterfeit products with authentic products.[1] Customers receiving poor quality products or an otherwise poor consumer experience inevitably blame the brand.

---

1. Hoffower, H. (March 29, 2018) *Fake products sold by places like Walmart or Amazon hold risks of everything from cyanide to rat droppings—here's how to make sure what you're buying is real*, Business Insider, https://www.businessinsider.com/how-to-find-fake-products-online-shopping-amazon-ebay-walmart-2018-3 [Accessed January 18, 2020]

Who are the diverted product sellers on Amazon?

There are two main types of sellers responsible for introducing diverted product to the Amazon Marketplace:

1. The online retailer that has no direct relationship with the brand: This seller may or may not be using a display name to disguise its identity. Most sellers are well versed in the so called "first sale doctrine," which generally affords the ability to resell genuine product without the brand's permission. We will discuss critical exceptions to this doctrine in Chapter 6.

2. The retailer or distributor that is authorized to represent the brand in brick-and-mortar channels, but uses a display name to sell on Amazon. It may disguise its online identity if the brand does not allow it to sell on Amazon.

Why do retailers and distributors get involved in diverted product?

Large, sophisticated product diverters sell diverted product because they can make a profit margin in selling the items, even if those margins are lower than what full price might generate in other channels. For these sophisticated sellers, the high demand and ease of sale (with little to no investment in the brand) for products on Amazon often compensate for differences in attainable margins. If you look at the largest grey market sellers/retailers of diverted product on Amazon, they treat every product as a widget. It does not matter the brand or category of product; if there is money to be made selling it, and there is demand for the product on Amazon, then there is an incentive for product diverters to source and sell these products.

However, it is important to understand the applicable dynamics at a deeper level. Remember the brand executive of the consumer-packaged-goods firm mentioned at the beginning of the book? If that brand's sales team offers volume discounts to its distributors or wholesalers, then the brand may actually be creating the margin opportunity through this volume discount. Take, for example, a brand's distributor, Dave, who has two options for purchasing pallets of product from a brand. Dave can buy 8 pallets per month for $10,000 per pallet, or he can get an additional 10 percent discount if he instead purchases 10 pallets at $9,000 per pallet.

OPTION A: Dave buys the 8 pallets for $10,000 per pallet, and sells them for $15,000 per pallet, making a profit of $5,000 per pallet, or a total of $40,000.

	EXPENSE	SALE	PROFIT
	8 pallets @ $10,000	8 pallets @ $15,000	Each pallet = $5,000
TOTAL	$80,000	$120,000	$40,000

Table 1: Total profit for a non-diverting reseller

OPTION B: Dave buys those extra 2 pallets to get the brand's volume discount. As a result, Dave buys each pallet at $9,000 per pallet, but can sell the 8 pallets as planned to his regular customers at $15,000 per pallet, making $6,000 in profit because of the volume discount. Dave then can divert the additional 2 pallets to an online seller who will pay cash up front. Even if he diverts the extra pallets at a lower cost than he sold the others—for $12,000 per pallet—he would still clear $3,000 of profit margin per pallet, or $6,000 total margin on the 2 extra pallets.

	EXPENSE	SALE	PROFIT
Standard sale	8 pallets @ $9,000	8 pallets @ $15,000	Each pallet = $6,000
PLUS	2 pallets @ $9,000	2 pallets @ $12,000	Each pallet = $3,000
TOTAL	$90,000	$144,000	$54,000

Table 2: Total profit for a diverting reseller

To make matters worse for the brand, these 2 pallets of diverted products are likely to be advertised online at a price much lower than what the brick-and-mortar retailers are prepared or able to offer for the units they have purchased. In total, Dave made $54,000 in total profit margin (8 x $6,000 + 2 x $3,000), instead of $40,000 (8 x $5,000), by buying 2 extra pallets destined for diversion. With limited holding costs (because the diverted inventory was sold for cash as quickly as possible), Dave made 35 percent more margin by participating in diversion. And because he was already buying 8 pallets, it was not hard for him to divert 2 additional pallets unnoticed by the brand (compared to an online seller who would have to contact the brand directly for the opportunity to buy 2 pallets and at a price per pallet that would be far higher for a small sale).

The larger a customer that a distributor or retailer is to the brand, the easier it is to hide and divert a few extra pallets of product. For example, if the distributor sets up its own disguised third-party seller account on Amazon designed to fill a demand for 2 pallets of product a month, it is much easier for that distributor to get those 2 pallets from the brand if it already buys 20 pallets for other channels than if the distributor were a smaller player buying only one pallet initially from the brand, and now wanting to triple its purchase.

Where does diverted product come from?

Both Vorys[2] and Buy Box Experts[3] have spoken with many brand executives who believe they have addressed product diversion issues for their brands. Yet these executives are surprised when they see diverted product supply continue to pop up unexpectedly. How does this happen?

We view combatting product diversion as a constantly evolving cost of doing business. Just when the brand thinks it has closed product diversion pathways, a new opportunity emerges for the creative product diverter. As brands get bigger and add new channels, distributors, and retailers, new opportunities for product diversion also surface. These are some of the most significant, but certainly not the only, sources of diverted product:

1. SPECIAL PRICING AGREEMENTS (SPAs): Brands like selling lots of product, and clever intermediaries know how to convert that into an opportunity to negotiate lower prices on bulk purchases from the brand. Often a distributor will explain to the brand that it needs better pricing for a large purchase of product for internal use by an end customer. For example, a company needs 800 laptops for its sales team, so the distributor tells the brand it needs special pricing for 1,000 laptops, or else the

---

2. Vorys eControl, https://www.vorysecontrol.com/ [Accessed January 18, 2020]
3. Buy Box Experts, https://www.buyboxexperts.com/ [Accessed January 18, 2020]

brand will lose the deal to a key competitor. The brand comes back with aggressive price discounts of 40–50 percent (or even more), helping the distributor to close the deal for 800 laptops, but also sneak an extra 200 laptops at unusually low prices, which the distributor can now divert at sizable margins.

This is simple math: if the size of the discount is under 15 percent, it is hard to middle the business, or create enough margin opportunity to buy excess inventory and divert it profitably. But, when discounting grows well above 20 percent from any normally available discounts, the opportunity to overbuy and subsequently divert product becomes quite apparent and financially desirable for intermediaries. If the brand is not doing any spot checks to verify quantities and pricing with the end customer, then the distributor may keep defrauding the brand.

2. VOLUME DISCOUNTS: Outside of SPAs, many brands offer volume discounts to distributors that buy more product. If the discount becomes big enough, the distributor will buy extra inventory just to qualify for the full discount and then divert the excess. Naturally, the distributor is then incentivized to find grey market sellers that want the excess inventory. Soon enough, a permanent trade relationship is built between the distributor and the grey market seller at a clear disadvantage to the brand.

Sometimes, a volume discount is offered to authorized sellers by a brand's salesperson because they need to sell a lot more volume to hit their own sales quotas. If the brand is not verifying the destination of product and terms of sale closely, this sort of behavior can go undetected, resulting in the salesperson calling preferred clients saying, "I need a favor; you need to buy extra inventory from me this month so I can hit my number. Help me, and I will get you a bigger discount." In this situation, the preferred seller has excess inventory and an incentive to unload it to companies that might not be authorized to buy the brand.

When this form of excess inventory gets sold by the brand, the brand usually views it as "accounted for" because it matches *current* end-user demand. Yet, it is really creating what we call shadow inventory; shadow inventory is held by distributors and retailers, still unsold to consumers, and in quantities unknown to the brand. The volume of product a brand sells to distributors and retailers does not always correlate with actual immediate customer demand; it may, instead, reflect an effort by the distributors and retailers to bulk up on the brand's product for some future sales opportunity. When the brand launches a new product, and cannot figure out why it is not selling as well as expected, it is often because shadow inventory is still being worked through by the distributors and retailers, thereby reducing their interest in carrying as much new product inventory.

3. PARALLEL IMPORTS/COUNTRY ARBITRAGE: Product is often designated for sale overseas. While this product may or may not actually end up physically in another country, it is made available in the home market for sale by a re-importer, either for wholesaling to an unauthorized reseller, or for retail selling by the re-importer themselves.[4] With regard to the U.S., there are dozens of ways that product can find its way back into the country through parallel imports, including:

a. A distributor creates a Shipper's Export Declaration (SED) form to show the brand that the product is being shipped overseas. However, the product is never shipped and remains in the U.S., where it will be diverted through wholesale and/or retail channels.

b. An overseas distributor ships overseas inventory back into the U.S. for sale in the U.S. While there may be multiple shipping charges, any wholesale pricing differences across countries may help to offset these additional shipping costs.

c. Products sent to Puerto Rico are sometimes sold at lower wholesale prices. But because Puerto Rico is still inside the U.S., the brand unfortunately is creating the opportunity for someone to buy the product in Puerto Rico, and resell it at a higher price in the mainland U.S., without having to pay any import duties.

---

4. For more details on these techniques, see deKieffer, D.E. (2010) *Underground Economies and Illegal Imports*, Oxford, Oxford University Press

This opportunity for arbitrage can be, and frequently is, leveraged by the opportunistic seller.

d. Any specialty channel (like duty-free shops or off-shore oil rigs) provides an opportunity for product to get lost due to less stringent inventory controls than those found through normal retail channels.

e. Charitable organizations can be the unwitting source of diverted product by not always sending brand-donated products to the countries where the products were intended, or by choosing to sell product to generate more flexible cash.

4. RETAIL ARBITRAGE: Retail arbitrage refers to the act of buying products in your local retail stores and then selling those same products through online marketplaces for a profit. The most reliable source of products is generally the clearance racks of large retail stores.[5] Such efforts typically play out in three ways:

a. Approved short-term retailer discounts, which create an opportunity for anyone to source products at prices low enough to make money reselling on Amazon.

b. Closeout pricing, which results in older inventory showing up on Amazon in large quantities. For example, an Amazon 3P seller can go to a brick-and-mortar store, purchase all of a brand's water bottles that store has in stock on clearance for $5 for a two-pack, and resell the packs on Amazon for nearly $20.[6]

c. Wholesale or retail pricing differences across international channels.

5. Grant, R., (February, 19, 2018) *Retail Arbitrage: A Complete Guide for Beginners* (*Amazon FBA 2019*), Online Selling Experiment, *https://onlinesellingexperiment.com/retail-arbitrage-2/* [Accessed January 18, 2020]
6. Siegel, R. (Feb. 8, 2019,) '*Flesh and blood robots for Amazon': They raid clearance aisles and resell it all online for a profit*, Washingtonpost.com, https://www.washingtonpost.com/business/economy/flesh-and-blood-robots-for-amazon-they-raid-clearance-aisles-and-resell-it-all-online-for-a-profit/2019/02/08/f71bff72-2a60-11e9-984d-9b8fba003e81_story.html [Accessed January 18, 2020]

5. AD SPECIALTY/SAMPLING COMPANIES: These firms acquire heavily discounted products from brands for the indicated purpose of providing the products as samples in channels that brands may have difficulty otherwise reaching. Brands that sell grocery and beauty products commonly use sampling companies to demonstrate their products in retail outlets where the brands do not otherwise have easy or local access. While brands see value in this marketing effort, dishonest sampling companies are able to acquire significant product volume at low prices—a recipe for disaster if the intention is to sell the product as diverted inventory.

6. SOURCING FROM MULTIPLE RETAILERS: This hard-to-detect approach can play out in a couple of different ways. First, a sophisticated reseller may contact many different retailers to ask each to divert a small amount of inventory to the reseller. By aggregating small amounts across many locations, it is much harder for brands to identify any particular retailer with an unusually high increase in wholesale orders. Alternatively, the company seeking to access large amounts of product for diversion may set up one or more storefronts under different names, and get the brand to sell to each storefront (potentially in completely different geographical locations). If the locations of these new storefronts are not particularly convenient for the brand to conduct onsite inspections, the storefronts may serve as effective fronts for sourcing inventory to be diverted for a long time.

7. PRODUCT SOURCED FROM RETURNS: This is often a completely unmanaged channel for brands. A retailer may negotiate a credit on returned products up to a certain level—for example, up to 2–3 percent of the retailer's inventory amount. When physical product is returned to the retailer, the brand simply pays the credit, but never checks to see where the product went. That product gets reinserted into retail trade, typically under a different seller name. If the retailer is large enough, even a 2 percent return credit creates significant volume of physical product. Because the inventory is already addressed on the brand's financial books as a return-related credit, the brand has no idea

the returned inventory exists, or where it might have been diverted. Adding to this problem, reverse distributors work with these retailers, offering bulk purchases of returned products. These distributors will do the necessary cleaning and repackaging to convert damaged or used product into apparently new-condition product that is then resold on a wholesale or retail level.

8. RETAILER PRODUCT CLOSEOUTS: When a retailer seeks to get rid of slow-moving inventory (especially product that the brand does not want back or allows to be returned for credit), the retailer often sells the product at heavily discounted retail prices, allowing anyone to buy these items and make them available for resale online at a large enough margin to make this worthwhile.

9. RETAILER LIQUIDATIONS/SURPLUS AUCTIONS: Overstock product may be purchased from retailers by liquidation specialists who then make the product available to auction bidders. The successful bidders are then free to advertise the product for sale at prices determined by them. Further complicating this channel is the ease with which stolen or counterfeit product can be commingled with liquidated inventory, resulting in additional headaches for brands attempting to maintain consistency of messaging and brand management.

10. MANUFACTURING PLANT MAKING EXTRA UNACCOUNTED-FOR PRODUCT: Such third-shift, or midnight-run, product is essentially otherwise authentic product made outside of the production times dictated by the brand. For example, a brand owner can outsource the manufacture of its products to foreign contractors. If a buyer orders 20,000 units of the product and the contractor fills the order during two day shifts, the contractor might then produce an extra 10,000 units during a night shift and divert those without the brand's knowledge and without a specific order from a buyer.[7] If the brand does not do spot checks, it is very easy for the manufacturer to become a reliable

7. Parloff, R. (Apr. 26, 2006) *Not exactly counterfeit*, Fortune.com, https://archive.fortune.com/magazines/fortune/fortune_archive/2006/05/01/8375455/index.htm [Accessed January 18, 2020]

source of large amounts of product that is hard to tell apart from the brand's authorized inventory.

11. VENDOR CENTRAL ACCOUNTS FROM DISTRIBUTORS/ RETAILERS: Amazon 1P offers Vendor Central accounts to companies that are not brand owners. In this way, distributors or large-scale diverters can offer to wholesale inventory to Amazon 1P. Because Amazon 1P will not reveal to a brand owner where else it is alternatively sourcing 1P inventory, the brand may find itself in competition with others for Amazon 1P's wholesale business on its own product. It may also find itself unable to sell product direct to Amazon 1P because Amazon 1P can buy the product for less from a diverter. Buy Box Experts has seen large 3P sellers sell large quantities of diverted product to Amazon 1P through Vendor Central, as it is easier for these companies to move large amounts of diverted inventory in a single sale to Amazon 1P, than it is for them to try to sell one unit at a time through a third-party seller account, using the Seller Central platform.

Amazon used to have a program called Vendor Express through which it offered large numbers of distributors and retailers the opportunity to sell products to Amazon 1P. Although Amazon ended this program in early 2018, it allowed practically anyone to sign up for a Vendor Express account. Now, wholesalers must get an invitation from Amazon 1P for a Vendor Central account; while this is certainly more difficult, it still permits large diverters to sell products to Amazon 1P.

Product diversion is not likely to ever go away, and the Amazon Marketplace is likely to remain a key U.S. destination for diverted product for the reasons explained in this chapter. Nevertheless, each brand has the opportunity to raise enough roadblocks in the path of product diverters to motivate them to stop selling the products. As most product diversion is generated by misaligned incentives across salespeople, distributors and retailers, it is the brand's executives who can identify and remove these misalignments (even if it causes some short-term pain) and who will secure the brand's equity in the long term.

While product diversion is an addressable issue, some brand teams are not prepared to make the significant investment of time and effort to do so, causing them to walk away from Amazon.

Case Study: Brand abandons the Amazon channel altogether

BUSINESS CHALLENGE: In July 2016, after years of attempted negotiations with Amazon, the shoe brand Birkenstock chose to walk away from the Amazon channel by no longer supplying Amazon 1P with product and making clear that it did not authorize any third-party sellers to sell its brand on Amazon. Frustrated by its inability to get Amazon to remove endless counterfeit listings[8] and to eliminate unauthorized seller activity, Birkenstock USA CEO David Kahan wrote in a note to Amazon: "The Amazon Marketplace, which operates as an 'open market,' creates an environment where we experience unacceptable business practices which we believe jeopardize our brand ... Policing this activity internally and in partnership with Amazon.com has proven impossible."[9]

SOLVING THE ISSUE: The choice that Birkenstock made may feel like the right approach once a brand has thrown its hands up in the air in disgust, but unfortunately, it leaves the brand significantly exposed on such a large channel. No one other than the brand is going to police counterfeits or ensure branding content is correct. And so, the problem continues.

OUTCOME: When Birkenstock made this decision, there were scores of third-party sellers listing Birkenstock product on Ama-

---

8. Bain, M. (July 23, 2016) *Birkenstock says Amazon is rife with counterfeits: How to avoid getting suckered into buying them,* Quartz, *https://qz.com/738620/birkenstock-says-amazon-is-rife-with-counterfeits-how-to-avoid-getting-suckered-into-buying-them/* [Accessed January 18, 2020]

9. Levy, A. (July 20, 2016) *Birkenstock quits Amazon in US after counterfeit surge,* CNBC, *https://www.cnbc.com/2016/07/20/birkenstock-quits-amazon-in-us-after-counterfeit-surge.html* [Accessed January 18, 2020]

zon. It is not clear how many of the items are legitimate or counterfeit products, and the quality of listings varies significantly.

The effect of lower advertised prices on the Amazon channel has inevitably caused problems for Birkenstock with its brick-and-mortar distributors and retailers. Long-term, the brand will lose equity because no one is focused on the Amazon channel issues. The larger the brand, the more risk the Amazon channel may create if the channel remains unmanaged by the brand.

We see this situation as a warning sign—all brands must have an active channel strategy on Amazon, whether controlling branding and listing quality, controlling distribution, mitigating arbitrage opportunities or actually actively selling 1P or 3P in the channel. Today, Birkenstock's competitors enjoy an advantage on Amazon, as these other brands are potentially able to get more than their fair share of organic search and customer conversion, all because they choose to be active in this channel.

In sum, there are myriad ways products can be diverted, and creative unauthorized sellers are undoubtedly developing new ways as you read this. In Section 3, we examine what brands can do to reduce the impact of product diversion on their own distribution and brand equity.

HOW WE PROPOSE TO FIX THE PROBLEM

CHAPTER 4

A COMPREHENSIVE, MULTI-STEP APPROACH: THE MARKETPLACE FLYWHEEL™

Innovation is the specific instrument of entrepreneurship. The act that endows resources with a new capacity to create wealth.

—PETER DRUCKER

IN CHAPTER 2, we described the virtuous cycle, or Amazon Flywheel, that Amazon uses to drive its efforts to grow the Amazon Marketplace. Amazon's efforts have paid big dividends in terms of creating a huge Marketplace that brings together millions of sellers, hundreds of millions of customers, and still larger numbers of product listings. As a result, the media has celebrated Amazon's size,[1] its value,[2] and its overall impact on multiple industries.[3]

One effect of this growth is that the Amazon Marketplace has accentuated weaknesses and blind spots that brands faced long before it took off in size and popularity. For example, before Amazon, there was not a

---

1. Weaver, D. & Pettitt, J. (April 14, 2018) *A look at Amazon's extraordinary empire*, CNBC, *https://www.cnbc.com/2018/04/13/just-how-big-is-amazon.html* [Accessed January 18, 2020]

2. Desjardins, J. (January 3, 2017) *Amazon is now bigger than most brick and mortar retailers put together*, Business Insider, *https://www.businessinsider.com/the-extraordinary-size-of-amazon-in-one-chart-2017-1* [Accessed January 18, 2020]

3. Selyukh, A., Goldfarb, A. & Abid, A. (November 13, 2018) *How Big Is Amazon? Its Many Businesses in One Chart*, NPR, *https://www.npr.org/2018/11/13/666274605/how-big-is-amazon* [Accessed January 18, 2020]

huge consumer marketplace available where practically anyone could sell product; the ease with which one can show up on Amazon as a seller has motivated hundreds of thousands of people who otherwise would not be sellers to pursue the Amazon Marketplace as an opportunity to build a business without much upfront investment. Likewise, the ability to sell under a DBA name helps sellers disguise their identity, making it easier for them to sell without the brand's knowledge, especially when brands do not police their distribution and sales processes adequately.

Historically, a brand decided with which distributors and retailers it wanted to partner. Having done so, it sold a known amount of product to the selected distributors and retailers, while also providing marketing collateral that could be used in the retail setting. But today, with potentially hundreds of sellers sourcing inventory from locations unknown to the brand, and creating product listings with whatever content the sellers want to use, the impact of the Amazon Marketplace buildout has been ever more challenging for most brands.

While Amazon will most likely continue to use and develop its growth strategy as outlined in the Amazon Flywheel, there are effective ways for brands to use the Amazon Marketplace as a profitable channel that fits within their distribution strategies. For most brands, doing so will involve making significant changes to the way they do business in all channels. We outline these changes in Chapter 6. While this book focuses on the Amazon Marketplace, the development of more online marketplaces in the U.S. and internationally will require brands to make these changes for all channels to remain competitive and to bolster future growth.

Our model for addressing how brands can control their success in online marketplaces focuses on three key areas:

1. Branding governance,
2. Channel governance, which this book addresses in more depth later, and
3. Growth-based advertising.

BRANDING GOVERNANCE broadly describes a brand company's efforts to ensure that all online content that describes its brand and products is used in a manner consistent with all the other channels in which the brand company shares messaging with consumers. For the Amazon channel, brand control typically involves being proactive in loading product detail page content (including images, text, and video) and Amazon store page content before other sellers can do so. If done properly, the brand company will be able to ensure that the messaging of its brand is correct, current, complete, and consistent with all other channels.

As part of branding governance, we include CATALOG OPTIMIZATION as a key activity. This involves not only loading brand content that the brand company wants in place, but also addressing catalog issues caused by other sellers' data submissions, such as duplicate product listings, incorrect UPC codes, and listings created for variations of a product (also known as variational listings) whereby specific color or size combinations have been split away from the parent listing. (Usually a parent listing would be intended to contain all of the listings of product variations, e.g. a t-shirt in S/M/L sizes and available in red/blue/white). As a brand gets serious about maintaining a clean, updated Amazon catalog, someone at the brand must be responsible for monitoring these issues, as they are often caused by unauthorized seller submissions.

In the online marketplace setting, CHANNEL GOVERNANCE refers to the brand company's efforts to control which retailers can sell the brand online, and at what prices these retailers may advertise the products. Because Amazon is an open marketplace that allows practically anyone to sell product, it is challenging for a brand to ensure that it knows each reseller that is listing its products on Amazon. Because Amazon does not get involved in helping brands enforce their distribution agreements and policies, brands need to anticipate that, without actively monitoring and policing their brand themselves, the Amazon channel will eventually turn into a wild, wild-west environment. Left unchecked, unauthorized or unknown sellers can easily list the brand's products in ways that are inconsistent with those products in other retail channels and in a manner harmful to the brand overall.

Finally, GROWTH-BASED ADVERTISING relates to wide-ranging issues about how the brand is promoted on Amazon through paid advertising. If a brand implements an advertising program, it can generate more traffic to its product listings, giving it an exposure advantage over competitor brands. A brand could even advertise directly on competitors' listings and search terms (Amazon's three main advertising tools are Sponsored Products, Sponsored Brands, and Product Display Ads).[4] Because Amazon advertising is a form of paid traffic, someone has to fund the advertising efforts. Yet for many brands, efforts to drive traffic through advertising are not coordinated with channel control efforts, leading to wasteful situations where the brand spends money promoting itself on Amazon, only to feed unauthorized sellers with more sales. Such marketing efforts by the brand create the wrong sorts of incentives, motivating additional unauthorized sellers to add listings for the brand's products onto Amazon, and to enjoy the increasing sales of the brand.

In consideration of these three key strategic issues, Buy Box Experts has developed a model highlighting the combination of activities that brands need to undertake to build successful, long-term businesses on the Amazon Marketplace. We call this model the Marketplace Flywheel™ (Figure 2).

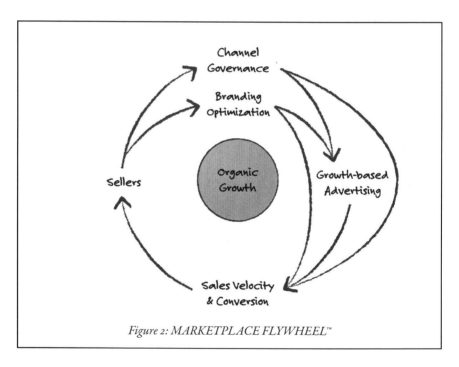

Figure 2: MARKETPLACE FLYWHEEL™

In our model, ORGANIC GROWTH constitutes the revenue growth of the specific brand's organically driven sales activities. As the brand generates SALES VELOCITY AND CONVERSION, new sellers become increas-

---

4. Visit Amazon's advertising page at *https://advertising.amazon.com/help* for more details

ingly interested in the brand, driving SELLER INTEREST. With more Seller Interest in the brand (both from authorized and unauthorized sellers), the brand's attention shifts to BRANDING OPTIMIZATION (how the brand is represented on Amazon, both through listings created by the brand, as well as listings created by any other third-party sellers). The brand also focuses on CHANNEL GOVERNANCE, where it not only picks and chooses by which retailers it wants to be represented on Amazon, but it also polices the channel to prevent unauthorized sellers from arbitrarily jumping on existing product listings and creating the potential for unwanted intrabrand competition and brand equity. Branding Optimization will generate a much cleaner catalog for the brand, making GROWTH-BASED ADVERTISING possible. While a brand can spend on Amazon advertising without a consistent brand presence across its Amazon catalog, Branding Optimization eliminates the significant waste that is typically present for brands that have not tidied up the branding in their Amazon catalogs.

Creating effective Channel Governance drives a number of beneficial outcomes. If a brand maintains effective Channel Governance, it is better able to secure a constant demand from approved sellers, and to stabilize its brand value. That Channel Governance will drive better Sales Velocity & Conversion of a brand's listings, as well as feed the opportunity for Growth-Based Advertising, so there is not unnecessary competition for the same keyword terms, or gaps where certain products are not being promoted by any of the resellers. Such efforts will improve the opportunities for Organic Growth.

We view the foundational component of a brand's successful Amazon strategy as Channel Governance. Only once the brand company has decided to get serious about controlling which sellers represent it on Amazon, are investments by the brand in a more optimized catalog and broader advertising campaigns going to pay direct, measurable dividends. Without Channel Governance, it does not take long for unauthorized resellers to control how the brand is presented to Amazon customers.

In summary, to counter the levers driving Amazon's growth, successful brands are using a combination of brand optimization, channel governance, and carefully managed traffic-generating advertising efforts to create organic sales growth on Amazon that complements well-coordinated offline channel activities.

CHAPTER 5

CHANNEL GOVERNANCE; PART I

You may not control all the events that happen to you, but you can decide not to be reduced by them.

—MAYA ANGELOU

FIXING CHANNEL GOVERNANCE is a two-part process that involves:

1. effective use of Amazon's existing programs, and
2. internal reflection by a brand about its own business structure, followed by development and execution of a strategy for exercising control over its sales channels.

In this chapter, we review the mistakes brand companies commonly make in attempting to control unauthorized sales and brand value, including relying too heavily on Amazon's existing programs or on baseless enforcement tactics. Chapter 6 will build on this to consider some solutions.

COMMON MISTAKES IN ATTEMPTS TO FIX CHANNEL GOVERNANCE

THE ECOMMERCE INDUSTRY is still mostly uncharted territory, so there are some common mistakes companies inevitably make in attempting to fix channel governance and stop the unauthorized sales of their products. Often these mistakes occur when companies opt for short-term, simple tactics over long-term or permanent solutions that require more upfront effort and internal evolution within a company. We discuss these common mistakes, as well as how Amazon has proposed to fix channel governance with varying levels of success.

Mistake #1: Relying on MAP policies to stop brand erosion

When faced with brand erosion and channel conflict, companies often turn first to MAP policies. Here is a typical scenario:

- An employee is designated to fix the problem of rampant online resellers harming brand value and begins to search online for solutions, quickly finding vendors that provide monitoring software to track violations and send MAP violation letters.
- The employee may also go to the company's traditional law firm or in-house counsel to prepare a MAP policy.
- The employee sends the MAP policy to the company's retailers and starts informing non-compliant retailers that they will be disciplined if violations continue.
- The retailers quickly point to numerous anonymous marketplace sellers listing far below MAP and ask why they should be held to MAP when these sellers are not.
- No one at the brand knows who the anonymous marketplace sellers are or how they are getting the products at issue.
- The employee tries to send violation notices through marketplace messaging systems to these anonymous sellers, but the sellers do not respond. In reality, the sellers do not care about the brand's threats because they know that they are under no legal obligation to follow MAP.
- The company must now decide whether to enforce its MAP policy against authorized sellers when doing so will be poorly received and will harm those relationships. Some companies decide to enforce MAP against some retailers but look the other way with respect to others, which exposes the company to legal risk, weakens the company's credibility with retailers, and can lead to further customer dissatisfaction. And others simply give up and retract their MAP policies altogether.

Mistake #2: Sending cease-and-desist letters to unauthorized sellers without viable legal claims

Certain non-legal vendors will convince brands that their unauthorized seller problems can be solved using threatening cease-and-desist letters through Amazon messaging, which are often sent without any legal basis. What these vendors often fail to disclose is that most high-volume, disruptive sellers have received many such cease-and-desist letters before and often refuse to comply with, or even acknowledge, these letters.

When a company is unable to take further action against these sellers, i.e., by filing a lawsuit, the sellers may become emboldened. They know that the company has no legal basis to stop them and will not be able to do anything other than continue to send ineffective letters.

Moreover, these types of letters can expose a company to legal risk and undermine a company's efforts to implement the necessary legal foundation to strengthen its legal claims against unauthorized sellers.

Vendors may proudly tout the numbers of letters sent and sellers removed, but they gloss over the fact that the removed sellers are likely small players that were never very disruptive in the first place, or that their targets simply changed their storefronts or moved to another marketplace. The reality is that the problems many businesses face are caused by large, sophisticated resellers that interfere with sales and disrupt brand value. Simply stated, companies need to do more than send baseless, scary letters to deal effectively with these unauthorized sellers.

Mistake #3: Submitting marketplace counterfeit tickets to remove unauthorized sellers

Some vendors take it a step further by representing to marketplace administrators that unauthorized sellers are selling counterfeit or otherwise infringing products when actually they are not. A common tactic is to message the sellers, asserting that they are not recognized. If the sellers do not respond or yield to the vendor's demands, the vendor will file a counterfeit or other infringement ticket on behalf of the brand without having an enforceable legal basis to do so. Brands using tactics like these have been punished by the marketplaces, even suspended from selling on the platforms. Moreover, a seller whose business is interrupted by a marketplace suspension may seek legal recourse against the brand and vendor for disrupting their businesses without cause.

Even if the products are truly counterfeit, this approach often results in the proverbial game of whack-a-mole. Brands may get a listing removed here or there, but they can never solve the larger problem so the sellers eventually return.

Importantly, brands cannot expect Amazon to interpret whether an unauthorized sale of an authentic product would violate the Lanham Act, 15 U.S.C. § 1051 *et seq.* (which codifies U.S. trademark law) or to take active steps to remove unauthorized sellers. For this reason brands need to resolve these issues themselves, and not look to marketplaces to do it for them.

Mistake #4: Measuring the wrong data

When brands make these mistakes, they often end up focused on data that has no bearing on business success. For example, brands may incorrectly focus on the number of sellers they have had removed, or the number of MAP violation letters they have sent. These are vanity metrics that have no meaningful business impact. The metrics that matter for most businesses are the percentage change in sales made by authorized sellers, the percentage change in overall pricing policy compliance, decreases in customer complaints about product quality, and diminishing requests for price concessions. If these are not improving, then your company should re-evaluate its strategy.

These mistakes highlight the need for companies to execute a comprehensive strategy that provides the necessary control over authorized sellers through channel governance practices and also an appropriate legal basis to take action against unauthorized sellers.

HOW AMAZON APPROACHES CHANNEL GOVERNANCE

AMAZON HAS IMPLEMENTED some programs that help some brands (though not all brands) control who sells their products on their Marketplace, including:

- a program called Brand Registry, which is commonly misunderstood by brands as a tool for dealing with channel control issues;
- the process of brand gating; and
- a program called Luxury Beauty

It is important to understand that the policies and functionality that Amazon attaches to these programs is regularly evolving, based on feedback from brands and business choices by Amazon. So, the specifics below are based on current information as of December 2019.

Brand Registry

As we will discuss more in Chapter 7, Brand Registry is an Amazon program developed to help brands lock down catalog content and deal swiftly with intellectual property rights violations and counterfeit claims. However, when the program was introduced in 2017,[1] many brands thought they could use it to file tickets with Amazon to have unauthorized sellers removed from the brands' offers on the Amazon Marketplace. When Amazon realized that brands were using false claims of counterfeiting or intellectual rights violations, Amazon stopped accepting most of these tickets, and went so far as to remove brands' Brand Registry rights for repeated false claims.

Brand gating

Brands registered with Brand Registry can ask Amazon to "gate" their products. Although brands want to eliminate unauthorized sellers from Amazon, this is not Amazon's goal or in Amazon's business interest. Operating as an open marketplace that welcomes almost any seller to the platform, Amazon rarely eliminates all unauthorized sellers of a particular product. Instead, Amazon may, if it reaches an agreement with the brand, restrict the ability for third-party sellers to sell certain products by requiring sellers of the products to provide proof, such as invoices, that the products are legitimate. This is called gating.

---

1. Johnson, T, (Oct. 11, 2019) *Amazon Brand Registry: How does it work and is it worth it?* www.tinuiti.com, https://tinuiti.com/blog/amazon/amazon-brand-registry/ [Accessed January 18, 2020]

Amazon can gate a brand by reaching an agreement with the brand on which specific parts of its catalog will be restricted. It then sends out notices to affected existing sellers (including sellers that no longer have active inventory, but have inactive listings of that brand in their Amazon catalogs) prohibiting them from selling these products on Amazon without proof that they are legitimate. In the Amazon notices that both our firms have seen, affected sellers are usually told they can apply for permission to sell, subject to written approval from the brand, which is something most unauthorized sellers will not get. Although brands registered in Brand Registry may be able to decide whether additional sellers can add offers to the brand's listings, there is no functionality within that program to go back and remove existing sellers.

Amazon is most likely to gate brands of products that are ingested or applied to the skin because their unauthorized sale can pose a high risk of harm to Amazon customers (and Amazon's public perception). But even for these brands, the process of becoming gated can take months of negotiation with various levels of Amazon executives and completion of a litany of test buy orders to demonstrate the need for gating. Buy Box Experts worked with a brand that did manage to get this level of full gating in place. However, the gating was quietly removed by Amazon a year later, as though somehow the risk of future harm to Amazon customers had been fully eliminated.

A few high-visibility brands (e.g. Apple and Sonos) have succeeded in getting some of their catalog on Amazon gated completely so that Amazon 1P has only new-condition offers on their products in the listings. It is important to understand that these gating situations are extremely rare, and likely will be offered to only those 1 percent of brands viewed as the most strategic or desirable brands for Amazon 1P. Even Nike, which in 2017 managed to get Amazon to gate some of its catalog, found that the vast majority of SKUs remained ungated (and a complete mess from both the channel control and catalog control perspectives). The next year, when Nike's new line of products was not gated, there was channel control noise all over again for the brand. Finally, in late 2019, Nike decided to completely stop selling products on Amazon.[2]

BOTTOM LINE: Gating is not an option made available to the vast majority of brands on Amazon. In running an open marketplace, it is not in Amazon's best interests to gate brands on command. Only with very senior Amazon executive involvement have brands gotten meaningful gating permissions, and even then, the gating didn't always remain permanent.

Luxury Beauty

In 2013, Amazon introduced the Luxury Beauty program.[3] If beauty brands were invited by Amazon 1P to participate in this program, Amazon 1P would remove all new-condition offers of the brand's products from other sellers in exchange for the brand providing Amazon 1P with a consistent supply of product. Given the vast distribution of beauty products and the difficulty in controlling their sales, many brands take advantage of this program for its gating option. And in most cases, Amazon 1P remains willing to respect the brand's Manufacturer's Suggested Retail Price (MSRP) or MAP policy.

Interestingly, some beauty brands have passed on the Luxury Beauty program, instead using some of the other channel control techniques mentioned in this book (and bearing the cost associated with them) to clean the channel themselves, and remain 3P sellers. While this approach requires more time and expense, brands with the available resources may prefer to have increased control over inventory and selection.

BOTTOM LINE: While we have not seen the gating functionality of the Luxury Beauty program offered to brands in other categories, the trade-off is a significant strategic decision: enabling Amazon 1P to become the exclusive seller of your brand on Amazon, versus managing channel control yourself. Making this decision requires the brand to examine its pain points, existing distribution arrangement, sales goals, and other factors unique to the brand's situation to determine how to proceed.

---

2. Bursztynsky, J. (Nov. 15, 2019), *Nike just 'tip of the iceberg' of companies ditching Amazon and selling directly to consumers*, CNBC, https://www.cnbc.com/2019/11/15/armstrong-nike-just-the-start-of-firms-ditching-amazon-to-sell-direct.html [Accessed January 18, 2020]

3. Adams, R. (October 10, 2013) *Amazon's Luxury Beauty Store Is Exciting News For Cosmetics Lovers*, Huffington Post *https://www.huffpost.com/entry/amazon-beauty-store_n_4076805* [Accessed January 18, 2020]

CHAPTER 6

CHANNEL GOVERNANCE; PART II

Having a great idea for a product is important, but having a great idea for product distribution is even more important.

—REID HOFFMAN

WHILE AMAZON OFFERS programs to support brands' ability to protect their brand equity and brands need to be proactive in participating in these programs, the responsibility for managing brand rights still falls squarely on the brands. Far too many brands do not have an appropriate strategy in place to do this, resulting in an Amazon customer experience that diverges from the brand's desired experience across all channels. This chapter explains the factors that influence a tailored, comprehensive strategy, the need for internal alignment within the brand throughout the process of developing and enforcing the strategy, the key components of a successful online sales control program, and the importance of creating a program in accordance with applicable laws.

THE NEED FOR A TAILORED, COMPREHENSIVE STRATEGY

THE VAST MAJORITY of threats to brand value arise from a lack of channel control and the cyclical effect it has on product diversion: heavily intermediated and uncontrolled distribution, which leads to insecure channels, which leads to product diversion, which soon gives rise to the presence of grey market online sellers against whom the company has no ability to take efficient enforcement actions, which leads quickly to diminished brand value.

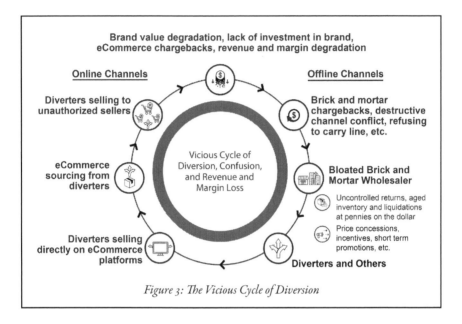

Figure 3: The Vicious Cycle of Diversion

To preserve brand value and be positioned for sales growth in the age of eCommerce, a company must effectively design and execute a comprehensive strategy that provides a foundation for control over both authorized and unauthorized sellers. Authorized sellers are those that purchase products from the brand or from authorized distributors, while unauthorized sellers are those that obtain a brand's products through diversion, theft, and other means. As noted in Chapter 5, attempts to address online sales challenges through half measures will, at best, be inefficient and ineffective, and will, at worst, thwart sales growth, harm authorized channel partner relationships, and expose the brand to legal risk.

Generally, brands that are achieving eCommerce success have strategies that include the following components:

1. Implement an online marketplace distribution strategy
2. Implement channel controls through an authorized reseller program
3. Understand authorized product differentiation

4. Implement an effective and legally compliant MAP policy, if desired.

5. Efficiently and effectively enforce against disruptive authorized and unauthorized sellers

6. Identify the root causes of eCommerce disruption and implement business changes necessary to mitigate them

THE NEED FOR ALIGNMENT

WHILE THIS CHAPTER will address each of these components in turn, we must first emphasize the importance of obtaining internal alignment and buy-in from key stakeholders—leaders in eCommerce, sales, marketing, customer service, legal, and other executives—at all points in the process. Without enterprise-level alignment, your brand's control strategy will not be optimized.

Further, achieving control in the eCommerce age is not a one-size-fits-all proposition. There are many options for how programs are structured, and many "buttons" that a brand can push to address its online sales challenges. The key is for company leaders to work together to determine the strategy that will work best for the company based on its products, industry, brands, and other business considerations.

Recognition of a problem

Development of a solution begins with recognition that there is a problem. If all key stakeholders do not recognize and understand the nature of a brand's online sales problem, it will be impossible to obtain buy-in for the business changes necessary to address the problem. To this end, key stakeholders must conduct an internal business analysis, considering the following questions:

1. What are our current pain points, e.g. unauthorized sellers, diminished brand value, lack of growth or distribution issues?

2. What metrics are most meaningful to our business, e.g. removing unauthorized sellers, increasing sales, reducing channel conflict?

3. What is our current distribution strategy—both in brick-and-mortar channels and online? Is it optimal for achieving our goals?

4. What is the nature and extent of any existing policies or procedures governing the resale of our products? Do our channel partners understand our rules regarding sales on online marketplaces?

5. What is the number and nature of unauthorized sellers facing the company and have there been any past efforts to remove them?

6. What are our budget realities?

7. How should ROI for our strategy be measured, e.g. permanent removal of unauthorized sellers, increased sales, increased margins?

As part of this internal business analysis, stakeholders also benefit significantly from education regarding the nature of online marketplaces and the threats facing the brand. This education can help stakeholders understand the consequences of failing to evolve to meet the new challenges in the age of eCommerce. Both authors have found in their experience working with hundreds of brands that an onsite educational meeting with key internal stakeholders of the brand is a critical first step to framing and obtaining alignment around the best strategy in today's market.

Alignment on a strategy to solve the problem

After achieving alignment on the nature of the problem and the need for a solution, brands must set their solution strategy. Key stakeholders should analyze all available options and develop a customized, comprehensive strategy for solving the company's unique issues. There are many options for addressing these problems. Importantly, different problems require different strategies, policies and procedures, and what works for one brand will not necessarily work for another. Brands must evaluate their options, speak to experts in the field, including their legal counsel, and discover which approach makes the most business sense for their unique situation. Careful thought must be given to the nature of the products at issue, current distribution methods, and other business realities. Brands should be incredibly wary of any vendor that suggests their technology or "proprietary" tactics will alone solve the problems.

Alignment on executing the strategy

Once there is a shared understanding of the problems facing the company and an agreed legally compliant strategy in place, the key stakeholders will need to remain aligned throughout execution of the strategy, even when difficult business decisions must be made. Further, key stakeholders must be committed to the strategy for the long-term benefit of the brand and must lead in communicating the reasons for the program to their teams and training affected parties on new policies and procedures.

COMPONENTS OF A COMPREHENSIVE, SUCCESSFUL SOLUTION

Component 1: Implement an online marketplace distribution strategy that will support your commercial goals

Companies need to be thoughtful in implementing an online marketplace sales strategy that will enhance, rather than harm, their ability to protect and grow their brands. There are many different factors that must be weighed in determining the best approach for each marketplace and for each company. However, one widely applicable best practice is to limit each marketplace to one authorized seller, or if absolutely necessary, a small number of trusted sellers that will be appropriately motivated to protect and grow the brand in the channel. This allows the brand to ensure all of its products sold online are subject to its quality controls, implement tracking mechanisms for its products sold online, and effectively monitor authorized online marketplace sales. Other approaches, e.g. allowing large numbers of marketplace resellers, often thwart sales growth, and dilute both brand image and value.

When selecting which retailers will be authorized to sell on online marketplaces, companies should consider a retailer's level of expertise with respect to marketplace sales, history of compliance with the company's policies, working relationship with the brand, and willingness to abide by the company's quality control standards. Online marketplace sellers should be trusted partners, working in tandem with the company to grow and protect the brand through the channel.

Component 2: Implement an authorized reseller program

Implementing an authorized reseller program is critical to ensuring that authorized sellers understand and abide by the brand's rules regarding where, to whom, and how products may be sold in an authorized fashion. These fundamental channel controls, which can be conveyed to channel partners by contract or via policies, should be applied to all sales channels and at all levels of distribution. In other words, they should reach both authorized sellers that buy directly from the brand and authorized sellers that buy from distributors (and have no direct relationship with the brand).

The following are key aspects and procedures for an effective authorized reseller program for a company selling through two-step distribution, although the specifics of each will depend on the company's existing business structure and needs:

1. The company sells products only to authorized distributors and authorized retailers with whom it has entered into authorized distributor or authorized retailer agreements or to whom it has provided authorized distributor or authorized retailer policies.
2. Authorized retailers are permitted to sell only to end users.
3. Authorized distributors are permitted to sell only to authorized resellers, who have entered into authorized reseller agreements with the company or, alternatively, to whom the authorized distributor has provided the company's authorized reseller policy.
4. Authorized resellers may sell online only after receiving the company's permission and then only on websites expressly approved by the company.
5. Resellers who violate the authorized reseller policy are subject to the brand enforcing its policy.
6. If the brand cannot reach a business resolution with the offending authorized reseller, the offending reseller's authorized status can be revoked and the reseller can be placed on a 'do not sell' list that is communicated to distributors. Once on such a

list, the reseller's inventory would no longer be authorized and would no longer be eligible for various benefits such as warranty repairs, returns and the like.

7. Enforcement efforts can then be undertaken using trademark claims against offending resellers who continue to sell the company's products.

Additional options for the types of agreements/policies and provisions to include in an effective authorized reseller program include the following:

Authorized distributor agreement/policy key terms

- Permitted to sell only to authorized resellers (as specifically defined in the agreement or policy).
- Cannot sell to any reseller on the 'do not sell' list.
- No online sales unless prior written approval is granted by the company.
- Required to exercise quality controls, including inspection requirements, product storage and handling requirements, reporting discovered defects, and other necessary requirements.

Authorized retailer agreement/policy key terms

- Permitted to sell only to end users.
- Sell online only on their own websites, subject to the authorized retailer terms and conditions.
- Acknowledgement that any limited rights in the company's intellectual property are revoked upon termination of authorized retailer status and the company may obtain injunctive relief in the event of continued use of the intellectual property.
- Required to exercise quality controls, including inspection requirements, product storage and handling requirements, reporting discovered defects, and other necessary requirements.

Authorized reseller agreement/policy key terms

- Permitted to sell only to end users.

- No online sales unless written prior approval granted by the company.
- Acknowledgement that any limited rights in the company's intellectual property are revoked upon termination of authorized reseller status and the company may obtain injunctive relief in the event of continued use of the intellectual property.
- Required to exercise quality controls, including inspection requirements, product storage and handling requirements, reporting discovered defects, and other necessary requirements.

Authorized online seller agreement key terms

- May only sell on those sites specifically identified and approved in advance by the company.
- May not sell anonymously or using a generic storefront name, and must provide legitimate contact information on the website or storefront.
- Acknowledgement that any limited rights in the company's intellectual property are revoked upon termination of authorized seller status and the company may obtain injunctive relief in the event of continued use of the intellectual property.
- Must implement additional quality control requirements that address quality control and customer service concerns in the eCommerce context.

Companies also often express concerns regarding certain distributors' or other customers' willingness to accept and abide by an authorized reseller program. However, the reality is, in our experience, the vast majority of customers respond favorably once they fully understand the reasons why the company is implementing the program.

The following are some useful talking points for communicating this information to distributors or retailers:

1. The company is committed to protecting and ensuring the long-term integrity of its brand by combating product diversion and the unauthorized sale of its products online.

2. Unauthorized sellers, particularly those selling anonymously online, sell damaged, defective, poor-quality, mislabeled, repackaged, and even counterfeit goods, which erode consumers' trust in the brand.

3. Negative consumer purchasing experiences lead to poor online reviews of products, which erode brand value, affect consumer purchasing decisions, and harm the brand and customers.

4. Distributors and retailers are also directly harmed by these negative effects as a result of decreased consumer demand for the company's products.

5. Left unaddressed, the sale of the company's products by unauthorized sellers will erode both brand equity through the company's authorized distribution channels and the viability of the brand.

6. To ensure that the consumers who purchase the company's products receive only high-quality products and have the best experience possible, the company will be implementing an authorized reseller program.

7. The authorized reseller program includes policies and agreements with all of the company's authorized distribution channel partners that describe the company's expectations regarding the ways that products may be sold, how products must be handled and cared for to ensure quality, and the service that must be provided to customers.

8. Pursuant to this program, authorized distributors will be permitted to sell the company's products only to authorized resellers. Authorized resellers will be permitted to sell only to end user consumers.

9. Under this program, authorized distributors will have no responsibility to police policy violations by their customers.

10. The new procedures are intended to support the company's relationships with distributors and retailers by protecting and enhancing the value of the brand to ultimately grow sales of products.

Case Study: Brand increases MAP compliance by implementing a holistic channel control strategy

BUSINESS CHALLENGE: An international consumer goods company found its products advertised at remarkably low prices on Amazon's Marketplace, leading to significant erosion of brand value and channel conflict. Around 80 percent of its products were being advertised at prices below MAP. The brand needed a plan to eliminate channel conflict, streamline its distribution on the Amazon Marketplace, and stop the erosion of its brand value.

SOLVING THE ISSUE: For the brand to gain control of its online sales, it needed a comprehensive, multifaceted strategy:

First, to enforce trademark violations against unauthorized sellers, which is a critical component of stopping unauthorized sales, the brand must own the trademarks or hold rights under a license. In this instance, the trademarks were registered to an owner in another country and the parties had to collaborate on trademark ownership issues and related brand protection efforts.

In addition to managing the trademark issue, the brand also needed to gain better control over its distribution strategy. By partnering with an exclusive authorized seller on Amazon, the company had only one partner to manage as opposed to many. This simplified monitoring and enforcement efforts against unauthorized sellers, and brought cohesion to its distribution model.

The brand also deployed thorough distributor and authorized seller policies, drafted with the help of outside counsel. Among other things, these policies notified distributors and retailers regarding channel controls—including where products could be sold online—and conveyed the brand's standards for how products should be handled and stored to ensure that only high-quality products reached consumers. These quality control standards provided a strong legal foundation against unauthorized sellers.

> RESOLUTION: Following implementation of this comprehensive approach, the percentage of MAP-compliant sales on Amazon reached all-time highs. At the end of 2017, only 22 percent of products listed on Amazon were advertised at or above MAP. By taking comprehensive and customized measures like those listed above, in less than 8 months, more than 99 percent of the products in the channel were advertised at a MAP-compliant price. The key to these successes was a comprehensive, legally compliant, custom control strategy designed to meet this brand's specific needs, coupled with an effective enforcement strategy.

Component 3: Understand authorized product differentiation

A critical, yet often overlooked, method of achieving control over online sales is by taking advantage of legal claims the company has against grey market or other unauthorized resellers. Importantly, it is generally legal to buy and resell genuine products without repercussion. This is the so-called first sale doctrine, and it is the primary defense raised by unauthorized sellers once targeted with enforcement.

The first sale doctrine—what is it?

A primary legal claim companies may have against unauthorized resellers in the United States is trademark infringement under the federal Lanham Act.[1] To prevail on this claim, a company must show that:

1. it owns a valid trademark;
2. the defendant used the trademark in commerce without the company's consent; and
3. the use created a likelihood of consumer confusion.

The first two elements are ordinarily straightforward to establish. The third, however, is complicated by a defense to liability under the Lanham

---

1. 15 U.S.C. § 1051 *et seq.*

Act called the first sale doctrine. This doctrine provides that it is generally legal for an individual to resell a trademarked item after it has been sold by the trademark owner in an authorized sale, even if the resale is without the trademark owner's consent. The underlying theory is that "trademark law is designed to prevent sellers from confusing or deceiving consumers about the origin or make of a product," and "confusion ordinarily does not exist when a genuine article bearing a true mark is sold."[2] Thus, a purchaser who "does no more than stock, display, and resell a producer's product under the producer's trademark" is protected by the first sale doctrine because those actions do not create "actionable misrepresentation."[3]

At first blush, the first sale doctrine would appear to bar a company from suing unauthorized sellers who are reselling the company's products as long as the products were originally sold by the company in an authorized sale. However, the first sale doctrine typically does not protect resellers who sell products without the services, benefits or quality controls that accompany products in authorized channels, particularly when those unauthorized sellers do not clearly explain these differences to consumers. This rationale is the basis for two exceptions to the doctrine that are central to a brand owner's ability to enforce against unauthorized seller activity.

EXCEPTIONS TO THE FIRST SALE DOCTRINE

Exception #1: Products sold by unauthorized sellers are 'materially different' from the company's authorized products

First, the first sale doctrine provides no protection when "an alleged infringer sells trademarked goods that are materially different than those sold by the trademark owner."[4] The basis for this exception is that, while there is ordinarily no possibility of consumer confusion when a resold product is *identical* to the product previously purchased from the mark owner, "[t]he probability of confusion is great . . . when the same mark is displayed on goods that are not identical but that nonetheless bear

---

2. *NEC Elecs. v. CAL Circuit Abco*, 810 F.2d 1506, 1509 (9th Cir. 1987)
3. *Australian Gold, Inc. v. Hatfield*, 436 F.3d 1228 (10th Cir. 2006)
4. *Davidoff & Cie., S.A. v. PLD Int'l Corp.*, 263 F.3d 1297, 1302 (11th Cir. 2001) (collecting cases from other circuits)

strong similarities in appearance or function."[5] For this reason, courts hold that the threshold for what constitutes a "material difference" must be kept low because "it is by subtle differences that consumers are most easily confused."[6]

In line with this principle, courts define a material difference as "any difference between the [trademark owner's] product and the allegedly infringing [product] that consumers would likely consider to be relevant when purchasing a product."[7] Importantly, differences do NOT have to be physical differences to satisfy this standard. Courts also hold that, if a mark owner shows that even a single material difference exists, there is a "presumption of consumer confusion sufficient to support a Lanham Act claim" and the alleged infringer can escape liability only if it can rebut the presumption by showing that "the differences are not of the kind that consumers, on average, would likely consider in purchasing the product."[8] If the trademark holder can establish that a material difference exists and that it could confuse consumers, then the first sale doctrine will not apply.[9]

Many recognized material differences are unique non-tangible customer benefits that are associated only with authorized products. For example, many companies have warranties that are limited to products purchased within authorized channels. In these cases, courts have found that the products sold by unauthorized resellers, who do not offer the same warranty, are materially different.[10] Similarly, many companies allow only those customers who purchase from authorized sellers to participate in promotional opportunities, helping them differentiate genuine products from those being resold by unauthorized sellers.[11]

Additional post-sale customer service and benefits can also constitute material differences. For example, products sold by unauthorized resellers

---

5. *Société des Produits Nestlé, S.A. v. Case Helvetica, Inc.*, 982 F.2d 633, 641 (1st Cir. 1992)

6. *Id.*; *see also Beltronics USA, Inc. v. Midwest Inventory Distrib., LLC*, 562 F.3d 1067, 1073 (10th Cir. 2009)

7. *Nestle*, 982 F.2d at 641

8. *Id.*; *see also Hokoto Kinoko Co. v. Concord Farms, Inc.*, 801 F. Supp. 2d 1013, 1038 (C.D. Cal. 2011)

9. See *Dan-Foam A/S v. Brand Named Beds, LLC*, 500 F. Supp. 2d 296, 317 (S.D.N.Y. 2007)

10. *Beltronics*, 562 F.3d at 1075-76

11. See *PepsiCo, Inc. v. Pac. Produce, Ltd.*, No. 99-1326-PMP-RLH, 2000 U.S. Dist. LEXIS 12085, at *4 (D. Nev. May 4, 2000)

without required post-sale technical assistance are materially different from those purchased through authorized channels where the seller is required to provide this service.[12]

Additionally, on a case-by-case basis, physical differences between genuine and diverted products can also be relevant. For example, resellers sometimes re-package diverted products (from bulk to individual sizes or by grouping popular combinations of products together as one item) to improve sales or deface a UPC or tracking code on the product or packaging to hide the source of their products. Such actions make the products non-genuine, and thus the Lanham Act prohibits sales of such repackaged or modified products.

Another difference between genuine and diverted products is that genuine products are almost always accompanied by additional information or literature about the product. Courts have generally recognized that differences in the instructions or literature accompanying a product can be sufficient to support a trademark infringement claim.[13] While these cases most frequently occur in the context of an unauthorized reseller offering products purchased in other countries, the principles have been extended to the sale of products originally intended for sale in the United States. For example, a company might provide additional product information through follow-up emails or mailings to customers who purchase from an authorized seller. Unauthorized resellers, because they lack a connection to the brand, cannot similarly provide this information to their customers. As a result, the purchasers of authorized products would receive a materially different product based on the accompanying information.

Exception #2: Differences in applicable product quality controls

A second, separate exception to the first sale doctrine exists when an unauthorized seller is reselling trademarked products that are outside of the trademark owner's quality control standards. For this exception to apply, the trademark holder must show that:

---

12. See e.g. *Beltronics*, 562 F.3d at 1073

13. *Original Appalachian Artworks, Inc. v. Granada Elecs. Inc.*, 816 F.2d 68, 72 (2d Cir. 1987)

1. it has established quality control procedures that are legitimate, substantial, and non-pretextual;
2. it abides by its quality control procedures; and
3. the unauthorized seller does not abide by the procedures and its sales of non-conforming products will harm the value of the trademark and create a likelihood of consumer confusion.[14]

Courts emphasize that it is not necessary for the trademark holder to have adopted the "most stringent" quality control procedures possible to invoke this exception, and it is also not required for the unauthorized seller to be reselling products of uniformly poor quality. This is because this exception protects a trademark holder's right to "control the quality of the goods manufactured and sold" under its trademark, and courts hold that resold products are not genuine if they are not subject to, and do not abide by, the mark owner's legitimate quality controls.[15]

Courts also hold that the first sale doctrine does not apply when an unauthorized seller interferes with a mark owner's ability to exercise its quality controls after its products have been sold to authorized sellers, for instance by preventing mark owners from being able to track defective products after they leave their possession and to conduct product recalls.[16] Such unauthorized sellers are not protected by the first sale doctrine because their actions "deprive[ ] the mark holder of an opportunity to exercise quality control."[17]

Unauthorized products sold outside of those quality control measures, or sold in a manner that interferes with them, can be deemed non-genuine and thus not protected by the first sale doctrine. This exception reflects and rewards the investment companies make in the quality of their products and in the trademarks they use to represent their brand.

Quality controls can include, among other things:

- requiring authorized sellers to conduct thorough inspections of products;

---

14. E.g. *Warner-Lambert Co. v. Northside Dev. Corp.*, 86 F.3d 3, 6 (2d Cir. 1996); *Iberia Foods Corp. v. Romeo*, 150 F.3d 298, 304 (3rd Cir. 1998)
15. *El Greco Leather Prods. Co. v. Shoe World, Inc.*, 806 F.2d 392, 395 (2d Cir. 1986)
16. See, e.g. *Zino Davidoff SA v. CVS Corp.*, 571 F.3d 238, 243-45 (2d Cir. 2009)
17. *Bel Canto Design, Ltd. v. MSS HiFi, Inc.*, 837 F. Supp. 2d 208, 229-30 (S.D.N.Y. 2011)

- storage, handling, and shipping requirements;
- an affirmative obligation to report discovered defects to the trademark owner;
- specialized training for authorized sellers;
- monitoring of authorized sellers and products;
- prohibiting anonymous online sales;
- vetting and regularly auditing all authorized online sellers;
- prohibiting commingling of inventory in marketplace warehouses; and
- prohibiting the resale of products that have been returned or repackaged.

To ultimately prevail on a trademark infringement claim, however, a company must not only identify a quality control that adds value to its product, such as ensuring breakable or liquid products are properly handled so they do not break or spill, but also be prepared to provide evidence that the control is legitimate and enforced.

This exception to the first sale doctrine protects companies that are dedicated to protecting the consumer, reinforcing the quality of their products and implementing appropriate quality controls to do so.

Component 4: Implement an effective and legally compliant MAP policy, if desired

Depending on the nature of the product, companies may also decide to implement an appropriate and legally compliant pricing or advertising policy, such as MAP, Minimum Resale Price (MRP) or MSRP, to protect brand value and alleviate channel conflict. In today's world of dynamic pricing algorithms, online advertised prices can be materially harmful to a brand's equity and overall value. However, companies should draft and implement these policies carefully and with the help of legal counsel to ensure compliance with federal and state antitrust laws.

Without the right policy in place across all sales channels, and a willingness on the part of the brand to enforce it, brand value can be eroded significantly. This, in turn, can result in major retailers refusing to carry certain products, listing suppression by online marketplaces and significant channel conflict. The key is to determine whether it makes sense for your company to implement such a policy and, if so, which will most effectively support your business goals.

Component 5: Enforce against authorized and unauthorized sellers

After the appropriate policies and procedures are in place, your brand can begin enforcement against authorized sellers who are violating your policies and unauthorized sellers who are infringing on your trademarks.

Key aspects of a successful enforcement process

Some key aspects of any successful enforcement process will include: (a) data and monitoring, (b) investigations to uncover seller identities, and (c) efficient and effective legally-backed enforcement.

a. Data and monitoring

Effective marketplace monitoring and consistent evaluation of key data is critical to prioritizing enforcement resources and achieving business success. Not all resellers are created equally. The focus should be on stopping those who are truly disruptive to your commercial strategy and brand equity, rather than indiscriminately pursuing enforcement actions any time products appear online.

The data most meaningful to prioritizing enforcement resources and driving real business value includes the following for each seller on each marketplace:

- Storefront and seller name
- Number of brand products listed
- Advertised price for each product
- Quantity of each product available
- Seller's quality rating
- Quality of the products sold, including whether they are selling damaged, outdated, or otherwise poor-quality products
- Whether test buys reveal the seller is selling damaged, defective, outdated, or otherwise poor-quality products
- Frequency of negative reviews

- Quality of the seller's listings

At the macro level, this data will inform the level of enforcement necessary to ensure a healthy online marketplace channel, including how many and which unauthorized sellers need to be removed to protect brand value and achieve stated business goals. On a seller-specific level, this data provides information useful for enforcement against individual unauthorized sellers, including:

- Do they have a material amount of negative seller feedback?
- Are they selling poor quality or fake products?
- Are they harming the brand's reputation in any way?
- Do they appear to be a professional reseller?

b. Investigations to uncover seller identities

Given that many unauthorized sellers operate anonymously, often taking great care to hide their identities, it is vital for effective enforcement to have a sophisticated seller investigation and identification process. Simply relying on marketplace messaging systems to contact unauthorized sellers is largely ineffective and can lead to disciplinary action from marketplace administrators. Instead, the individuals and businesses behind anonymous storefronts must be unmasked before they can be efficiently removed. Investigation teams leverage open source intelligence, advanced cyber investigation techniques, access to enhanced informational databases and, ultimately, the legal subpoena power to uncover the true identities of those persons and businesses engaged in unauthorized sales.

c. Efficient and effective enforcement

Once a company has developed a strategy to enact the necessary control over its channels and identified the offending unauthorized resellers at issue, the next step is to conduct effective enforcement. Any enforcement system should efficiently and permanently remove unauthorized sellers on a broad scale within realistic budget constraints. To do this, the company must develop an enforcement workflow that seamlessly combines technology, investigations and specialized legal enforcement to identify, target and permanently remove unauthorized sellers. The best workflows utilize a graduated approach that allows less expensive techniques to be applied across large volumes of sellers, while reserving advanced legal tactics for only the most troublesome and disruptive sellers.

As an initial matter, authorized sellers acting in violation of company policies (i.e., channel policies, MAP policies, and the like) can be dealt with in a business-to-business manner using the following methods:

- Business incentives/disincentives
- Education regarding brand policies
- Account termination
- Placement on a 'do not sell' list

Unauthorized sellers require a different approach. These sellers often believe their activities are protected by three "shields":

1. they believe what they are doing is legal in that they are protected by the first sale doctrine;
2. they believe that even if they are not so protected, the company will never uncover their identity; and
3. they believe that even if the company obtains their identity, it will not do anything about their misconduct.

To successfully stop grey market disruption, companies must implement an enforcement system that clearly demonstrates to unauthorized sellers why each of these three shields fails.

The most efficient broad-scale enforcement system begins by using strong monitoring technology to identify all unauthorized product sellers across the internet. While many monitoring companies can perform this function, the best technology identifies which sellers are actually disruptive. If a company has implemented a viable distribution strategy and has set up the appropriate foundation, as described earlier in this Chapter, all disruptive sellers can then be precision-targeted with forceful cease-and-desist letters that clearly explain why, as a matter of law, their conduct is illegal and not protected by the first sale doctrine. As an initial step, legal counsel, working with skilled cyber investigators, should obtain the sellers' identities. Once an identity is obtained, a physical cease-and-desist letter can be sent to the seller's home or business, again explaining why their conduct is illegal and, importantly, letting the seller know that they are no longer anonymous. Most sellers will either remove their products at this stage or attempt to negotiate a resolution. Finally, for the most persistent unauthorized sellers, more advanced legal strategies can be employed, including sending draft complaints, subpoenas, or filing lawsuits and seeking injunctions or money damages.

This type of graduated approach to enforcement allows a company to control costs and reduce the overall volume of unauthorized sellers while still maintaining the ability to use the litigation process against noncompliant resellers. Such a system operates best when it repeats each of these steps on a monthly basis.

By correctly implementing an effectively integrated, graduated monthly enforcement system, companies can realize steady reductions in the number of unauthorized sellers over time. In addition to permanently removing unauthorized sellers and curbing grey market disruption, a properly executed enforcement system also delivers valuable intangible benefits for the company, such as improving brick-and-mortar retailer satisfaction, ensuring the sale of high-quality products, and reducing consumer confusion across channels.

Case Study: Brand eliminates unauthorized sellers through suffocation of product supply

BUSINESS CHALLENGE: A mid-sized beauty brand found itself in a situation where it had over 100 unauthorized 3P sellers offering its products for sale on Amazon. The brand was not a 3P or 1P seller itself, but was particularly frustrated by the harm to its brand image being driven by these low-quality unauthorized sellers. To make things worse, there were issues with counterfeit products finding their way into various retail channels, so the brand naturally expected some of that product might be mixed in on the Amazon channel.

SOLVING THE ISSUE: The brand knew it needed professional help. It hired an agency to figure out how to regain control of the Amazon channel. The agency undertook a number of critical steps, including merging duplicate listings, optimizing the remaining listings, and filing tickets with Amazon to have bin checks of FBA inventory of the various unauthorized sellers. Those physical bin inspections identified widespread counterfeit issues.

So the agency and brand together made dozens of test buys, and filed the necessary tickets with Amazon to have the counterfeit listings removed. Eventually, the agency set up Brand Registry for the brand, making removal of future counterfeit products easier through the support team within Brand Registry.

As many brands have done, it sent out cease-and-desist letters to all the unauthorized sellers. While the majority of sellers heeded the letters and stopped selling the brand, a number of them remained. Next, the brand hired a law firm to identify applicable legal claims arising from the products being sold by the unauthorized sellers and sent letters outlining those claims to the remaining unauthorized sellers, threatening suit if the sellers did not remove their offers immediately. This step was very effective.

While the cease-and-desist process was underway, the brand launched a 3P seller account of its own, and eventually was able to garner at least 98 percent of the buy box. As a consequence, the brand's image on Amazon became much better aligned with its overall perceived value in the market.

RESOLUTION: While these legal procedures removed unauthorized sellers from the platform, the long-term solution did not kick in until the brand's executive team conducted a comprehensive review of every multi-unit order from retailers. The executive team found a number of large bulk purchases through both its wholesale B2B and consumer sites, purchases that did not equate with known retail sales. Once new sales policies stopped these types of purchases, most of the grey market supply for current and future unauthorized sellers evaporated almost completely.

> While this process of changing its channel distribution model resulted in a short-term loss of sales for the brand, the long-term effect was overwhelmingly positive, and lost sales were more than made up for on the Amazon channel through sales through the brand's own 3P account.

Component 6: Identify root causes of eCommerce disruption and implement business changes

In addition to enforcement efforts, brands may benefit from changes to their business practices to prevent or reduce product diversion. Keeping up with product diverters is a constant game of cat-and-mouse, including managing relationships with internal sales teams, distributors and retailers, many of whom may have motives that do not align with a brand's efforts to maintain brand equity across all its channels. There are a number of physical and operational changes that brands can make and best practices that brands can use to reduce the likelihood of being easy targets for sophisticated product diverters.

In sum, sophisticated product diverters and grey market sellers have historically relied on the first sale doctrine to defend their sales on Amazon as they rapidly build inventory. Brands also may be unknowingly creating incentives to encourage further product diversion. Fortunately, protective procedures based on emerging case law and sophisticated business controls are starting to be used successfully by brand executives to regain brand control and grow profitability online.

CHAPTER 7

CATALOG GOVERNANCE, INTELLECTUAL PROPERTY RIGHTS, AND COUNTERFEIT ISSUES

Online, offline, it's gotta be the same.

—ANGELA AHRENDTS, CEO BURBERRY

I N ADDITION TO low-quality product diverters, the open nature of Amazon's Marketplace has facilitated opportunities for counterfeiters to take advantage of a large consumer market.[1] In early 2019, Amazon went so far as to acknowledge this publicly, saying:

> *Under our seller programs, we may be unable to prevent sellers from collecting payments, fraudulently or otherwise, when buyers never receive the products they ordered or when the products received are materially different from the sellers' descriptions. We also may be unable to prevent sellers in our stores or through other stores from selling unlawful, counterfeit, pirated, or stolen goods, selling goods in an unlawful or unethical manner, violating the proprietary rights of others, or otherwise violating our policies. Under our A2Z Guarantee, we reimburse buyers for payments up to certain limits in these situations, and as our third-party seller sales grow, the cost of this program will increase*

---

1. Kaziukenas, J. (March 26, 2019) *Amazon Counterfeits Bottleneck*, Marketplace Pulse, *https://www.Marketplacepulse.com/articles/amazon-counterfeits-bottleneck* [Accessed January 18, 2020]

and could negatively affect our operating results. In addition, to the extent any of this occurs, it could harm our business or damage our reputation and we could face civil or criminal liability for unlawful activities by our sellers.[2]

Recognizing the complexity of handling millions of sellers, Amazon has created a variety of programs over the years to help brands better address counterfeit issues that can occur on the Amazon Marketplace.

We examine four initiatives and programs being used by Amazon to support brands' efforts to protect their intellectual property rights and fight counterfeit issues:

1. Brand Registry
2. Transparency program[3]
3. Test buy process
4. Utility Patent Neutral Evaluation procedure

1. BRAND REGISTRY

DEVELOPED TO HELP brands lock down content in the Amazon catalog and make it easier to seek Amazon's help in removing counterfeit offers, the Brand Registry[4] program is an important first step by Amazon to clean its catalog of undesired content and product listings.[5]

Prior to Brand Registry, which began testing in 2013 and was ultimately launched in its current form as Brand Registry 2.0 in 2017, a third-party seller would submit product listing data to Amazon's catalog. If that data was incorrect, incomplete, or inconsistent with the content that the brand wanted to be used for its product listings on Amazon, there were

---

2. *We could be liable for fraudulent or unlawful activities of sellers. Form 10-K*, p.14. Amazon.com, Inc., January 31, 2019. *https://www.sec.gov/Archives/edgar/data/1018724/000101872419000004/amzn-20181231x10k.htm* [Accessed January 18, 2020]

3. *Transparency*, Amazon.com, https://brandservices.amazon.com/transparency [Accessed January 18, 2020]

4. Brand Registry, Amazon.com, https://brandservices.amazon.com/ [Accessed January 18, 2020]

5. Dastin, J. (March 21, 2017) *Amazon to expand counterfeit removal program in overture to sellers*, Reuters, https://www.reuters.com/article/us-amazon-com-counterfeit-idUSKBN16S2EU [Accessed January 18, 2020]

not many suitable options for brands to update and control the content for listings of their own products. For brands that had no direct relationship with Amazon (either through Seller Central or Vendor Central), it was doubly frustrating as these brands had no suitable path for communicating with Amazon to notify it of deficiencies in the catalog.

Recognizing that high-quality data helps drive customer confidence and customer conversion, Amazon started testing the Brand Registry program. Under the program, brands could be given the ability to lock down most of the content for Amazon listings of products within their brand. Now a brand could ensure that its desired content for the product title, bullet points, product description, and certain product images were received into Amazon's catalog as the authoritative content that should be displayed ahead of any other sellers' contributions on these items.

In addition to protecting content, brands accepted into the Brand Registry program were also able to file tickets complaining about counterfeit products that the brands identified on Amazon.

By 2017, Amazon relaunched this program as Brand Registry 2.0,[6][7] allowing only registered trademark owners to apply for the program (a separate trademark number is needed in each country where the brand wants Brand Registry access). All earlier Brand Registry applications were voided, and brands had to re-submit paperwork for entry into this new program. Today, the program helps brands (or authorized Registered Agents of the brand) in three primary areas:

1. Locking down accurate brand content in the Amazon catalog;
2. Finding likely counterfeits and other IP violations across Amazon Marketplaces, and being able to file tickets on Amazon for quick removal of content violators; and
3. Requiring that new sellers seek permission from Brand Registry approved brands to create listings for the brand's products on Amazon.

6. Johnson, T. (Oct., 11, 2019) tinuiti.com, https://tinuiti.com/blog/amazon/amazon-brand-registry/ [Accessed January 18, 2020]
7. Lindsey, D. (Dec. 12, 2017) *What Is Amazon Brand Registry and What Do I Need To Know About It?*, Forbes, https://www.forbes.com/sites/forbesbusinessdevelopmentcouncil/2017/12/12/what-is-amazon-brand-registry-and-what-do-i-need-to-know-about-it/#1d611acf762f [Accessed January 18, 2020]

Sellers can no longer act on behalf of Brand Registry brands without the brand's knowledge. Furthermore, Amazon can confirm the brand's actions because the brand is associated with a registered trademark.

It is worth noting that just because a brand has been approved for Brand Registry 2.0 does not mean that the brand's catalog content in Amazon is automatically locked down. A key point often overlooked by brands is that the brand must submit the data into Amazon's catalog. That is typically done through a Seller Central account. This requires the brand either to:

1. work through a third-party seller that can submit the desired catalog content (with the third-party seller set up as a Brand Registry Registered Agent of the brand), meaning its content submitted on the brand's listings will be given authority in the Amazon catalog; or

2. set up its own third-party seller account for the purpose of submitting catalog content. Some brands will set up such an account not for selling, but simply for submitting and controlling catalog content.

BOTTOM LINE: We like the Brand Registry program for facilitating brands' efforts around content clean-up and counterfeit removal. However, it should not be used as a direct or indirect tool for cleaning up existing unauthorized seller activity.

2. TRANSPARENCY PROGRAM

FOR A COUNTERFEITER looking for fast-selling products to copy, published sales rank data on Amazon's product listings provides an attractive slate of target products. While the Brand Registry program has helped brands remove counterfeit listings from the Amazon marketplace, the Transparency program takes a more proactive approach—it is designed to help brands prevent counterfeit listings from first appearing on the marketplace.[8]

A brand can file a ticket with Amazon claiming that a seller is selling a counterfeit product, but Amazon typically requires the brand to do a test buy of the purportedly counterfeit product. For a brand faced with a seemingly endless number of counterfeiters, this whack-a-mole process never completely solves the underlying problem.

The Transparency program is designed to address counterfeiting by allowing only products with special Transparency numbering printed on the packaging to be sold on Amazon. A brand may register an individual SKU in the Transparency program and agree to print unique Amazon-generated numbers onto all units of that SKU for sale in all channels (i.e. all brick-and-mortar and online channels). Amazon charges the brand a fee (roughly $0.01 to $0.05, depending on the amount of Transparency numbers purchased) to generate all of these numbers. As a result, the brand must bear the cost of both the Amazon fee and the labor or production costs associated with printing the numbers on the products.

After a short period (typically no more than three months), all units of the impacted SKU sold on Amazon by any seller must have a Transparency number on its packaging. For sellers that use FBA (the Fulfillment By Amazon program), in theory, Amazon should not accept units of that SKU into its fulfillment warehouses that do not have a Transparency number. For sellers that fulfill orders themselves or use a non-Amazon fulfillment service, the seller is required to send Amazon a photo of each unit sent to a customer, so Amazon can verify that the appropriate Transparency numbers are on the item.

If every single unit of the SKU has an individualized Transparency number, it is difficult for a counterfeiter to introduce counterfeit product into the Amazon Marketplace (particularly in any large quantity). It is also difficult for a counterfeiter to fabricate Transparency numbers, as those numbers are unlikely to match the actual range of numbers provided by Amazon to a brand to apply to its units of that SKU.

---

8. Lunden, I. (July 10, 2019) *Amazon expands Transparency anti-counterfeit codes to Europe, India and Canada*, techcrunch.com https://techcrunch.com/2019/07/10/amazon-expands-transparency-anti-counterfeit-codes-to-europe-india-and-canada/ [Accessed January 18, 2020]

Remember that this program is used to remove counterfeit product, not to remove unauthorized sellers. Were an unauthorized seller to source units containing the Transparency numbers, that seller would still be able to sell them on Amazon. For brands that have unknown quantities of what we call shadow inventory (unsold inventory that is held by wholesalers, distributors and retailers), it can be challenging to determine how long of a transition period is needed before enforcing the legitimacy of product through Transparency numbers.

BOTTOM LINE: Although the program continues to be tweaked by Amazon, and although the cost of buying Transparency numbers or updating manufacturing procedures is relatively high, for some brands it can be justified if the cost of lost sales from counterfeits is noticeably higher. Brands that have only a small portion of their total distribution on Amazon may struggle to justify the cost of applying Transparency numbers to its products when a majority of units will never see the Amazon channel.

Case Study: Brand fixes counterfeit problem with Amazon Transparency Program

BUSINESS CHALLENGE: Late one night, the owner of a U.S.-based beauty brand (having several million dollars in sales a year on Amazon through both 1P and 3P accounts) discovered an unknown seller offering his brand of products and winning the buy box. Early the next morning, the unknown seller's offer disappeared. The next night, the unknown seller's offer appeared again at around 11:30pm, and disappeared again around 7:00am. In an apparent effort to avoid detection by the U.S. brand, this overseas seller was scooping up sales during hours when most U.S. sellers might not notice.

By doing a test buy, the U.S. brand owner discovered that this seller was selling counterfeit versions of its products. While the brand owner was able to get Amazon to remove this seller through the test buy process, it was frustrated when another seller immediately popped up under a different name selling the same counterfeit product. With the removal of each seller came the appearance of a new seller. With each new seller, the brand owner made a test buy, and found the same counterfeit product was being offered. During the six-to-seven day period that it took for the test buy to arrive, the counterfeiter continued to capture Amazon sales, harming consumers and brand value and detracting from the brand owner's 1P and 3P sales of legitimate product.

SOLVING THE ISSUE: Rather than continue this process, the brand owner started sending letters to the Amazon Brand Registry team and the general complaints email address at Amazon, each time copying his Vendor Manager. He repeatedly received notices stating that it was not Amazon's responsibility to manage the brand's distribution. The Vendor Manager got so fed up with the brand owner complaining about counterfeits that they removed the 1P offer on the listing, telling the brand owner that the brand needed to fix the counterfeit problem itself.

Eventually, the brand owner was introduced to the Amazon Transparency program, and the Customer and Brand Trust team that work with it. At a cost of about $0.15/unit to buy a unique Transparency number for each unit and to buy and apply a sticker with that number onto each unit, the brand owner calculated that this additional manufacturing cost was much lower than the lost sales he would suffer from future counterfeiters.

While Amazon does not favor gating to eliminate current or future sellers from seeking sales of specific products, Amazon's Customer and Brand Trust team was able to prevent any additional sellers from adding their offers on this brand's listings during a three-month period. During this period, the brand implemented manufacturing changes to add Transparency stickers to all newly produced units of its impacted SKUs. This period, known as the Operational Review Process, gave the brand time to make the necessary adjustments without having to deal with constant whack-a-mole removal of re-appearing counterfeiters.

> RESOLUTION: Today, with all units of this brand's products now labeled with Transparency stickers, the brand owner and Amazon are both able to ensure that only authentic versions of this brand are sold on Amazon.

In February 2019, Amazon rolled out the Project Zero initiative.[9] This program combined aspects of the Transparency and Brand Registry programs, and added features that make it easier for brands to identify and get counterfeit listings removed. At the time of writing it is only available by invitation and brands can apply to be waitlisted.[10] As the Project Zero initiative has not been rolled out beyond a small beta test with a handful of sellers, details of the exact mechanics have not yet surfaced.

3. TEST BUY PROCESS

BRANDS ALSO TYPICALLY have to conduct test buys to prove to Amazon that counterfeit versions of their products are being listed on Amazon. By conducting test buys, brands can examine products for signs of counterfeiting and report those findings to Amazon to expedite the removal of the listings.[11]

Given the ease with which some bad-apple sellers are able to disguise themselves over and over on Amazon under new seller accounts, fully removing sellers of counterfeit, patent, or trademark-violating products remains a big challenge for brand sellers and Amazon alike. Both authors have worked with brands that have spent tens of thousands of dollars on test buys, resulting in corners of their warehouses housing fake or illegit-

---

9. Steiner, I., *Amazon Launches Anticounterfeit Program Project Zero*, ecommercebytes.com, Feb. 28, 2019, *at* https://www.ecommercebytes.com/2019/02/28/amazon-launches-anticounterfeit-program-project-zero/ [Accessed January 18, 2020]

10. Gonzalez, G. (Feb. 18. 2019) inc.com, https://www.inc.com/guadalupe-gonzalez/amazon-project-zero-to-fight-counterfeit-products.html [Accessed January 18, 2020]

11. Bercovici, J. (from the March/April 2019 issue of Inc. magazine) *One entrepreneur's tale of his time in Amazon purgatory—and how he finally prevailed,* Inc., *at* https://www.inc.com/magazine/201904/jeff-bercovici/amazon-fake-copycat-knockoff-products-small-business.html [Accessed January 18, 2020]

imate product purchased from the Amazon Marketplace. This is because Amazon has required the brand to make a test buy of that product to obtain a test buy order number, which they need to present to Amazon's enforcement teams as physical proof to get the offer(s) removed, and the seller(s) punished.

The test buy requirements also can cause collateral damage to brands because Amazon is able to shut down accounts that appear to be abusing the Amazon refund policy by returning too many products. As a result, some brands spend significant money making test buys but cannot get refunds for fake or illegitimate products without risking the shutdown of their seller accounts.

BOTTOM LINE: Amazon often requires brands to conduct test buys to prove there are counterfeit versions of the products being listed on Amazon. Although the test buy process provides valuable information to the brand, it is not without cost to the brand.

4. UTILITY PATENT NEUTRAL EVALUATION PROCEDURE

FACED WITH YEARS of complaints from brands that other sellers were knocking off their products and selling on the Amazon Marketplace,[12] Amazon recently launched a new program to help patent owners combat infringing products—the Utility Patent Neutral Evaluation procedure. Launched as a pilot program in 2019, the program is designed to expedite a patent owner's process of getting infringing products removed from Amazon. Presently, participation in this program is by invitation only, but it has been reported that Amazon has invited some brands that have asked to participate.

Brands use patents to protect the innovative aspects of their products because patents give brands the right to exclude others from practicing the invention claimed in the patent. While the U.S. offers three types of patents (i.e., utility, design, and plant patents), the Amazon Utility Patent Neutral Evaluation procedure only allows brands to assert their utility patents. Utility patents are used to protect the structural and functional

---

12. Semuels, A. (April 20, 2018) *Amazon May Have a Counterfeit Problem*, https://www.theatlantic.com/technology/archive/2018/04/amazon-may-have-a-counterfeit-problem/558482/ [Access January 18, 2020]

aspects of a product, which are defined by the claims found at the end of the patent. Each patent claim includes one or more elements that make up the invention. For example, a brand may have a utility patent over a mug that keeps drinks hot, with claims that protect various innovative aspects of the mug, like the use of a new insulating material or a new type of seal on the lid.

Under Amazon's Neutral Evaluation program, a brand with a utility patent can submit an application to Amazon identifying the patent, one claim, and the accused product or products (identified by ASINs) that likely infringe that claim. Once Amazon receives the application, it sends it to every seller of the accused products on Amazon, at which point the seller can either participate in the evaluation process or Amazon will remove its listings. If the seller chooses to participate, then Amazon will send the application to a neutral patent evaluator, typically an attorney experienced in the type of patent dispute at issue.

The evaluator will decide if the patent owner is likely to prove that the accused products infringe the asserted patent claim. To do so, the brand must be able to convince the evaluator that the accused product includes each element recited in the asserted patent claim. For example, if the claim recites elements A, B, and C, then the patent owner must convince the evaluator that the accused products also have elements A, B, and C. Returning to the example of the coffee mug, if the asserted patent claim recites a mug having insulation made of material X, then the patent owner will need to prove that the accused product is a mug that has insulation made of material X.

The evaluation process is quick, but does have a cost. The brand and seller must each give the evaluator a deposit of $4000 to participate in the process. If the seller does not make this deposit, Amazon will remove its listings of the accused products; if the brand does not make the deposit, the evaluator will return the seller's fee and the process will end. The loser's deposit is used to pay the evaluator's fee at the end completion of the evaluation and the winner's deposit is returned.

The evaluation consists exclusively of written arguments, or legal briefs—neither side appears before the evaluator, and there is no opportunity for the brand and seller to gather information from each other through discovery. The evaluation process also moves quickly with the evaluator's decision being issued about four months from the date that the patent owner submits their application. The evaluator's decision will be either that the patent owner is likely to prove infringement or not likely to prove infringement. If the decision is that the patent owner is likely to prove infringement, Amazon will remove the listings of the accused products within about 10 business days of its receipt of the decision. If the accused products are not infringing, the process ends. There is no process for either side to appeal the decision to the evaluator or Amazon. If the parties settle the dispute before the evaluator has reached a decision, then the evaluator can retain up to $1000 of the fee and refund the rest to each side.

If a seller loses and later wants those accused products to be relisted on Amazon, it can attempt to obtain a court order that the accused product is not infringing or the patent is invalid or unenforceable. The seller may also seek to invalidate the patent through the U.S. Patent and Trademark Office's post-grant proceedings. Likewise, if a brand loses in the evaluation process, it can attempt to obtain a court order that the accused products are infringing, and Amazon will remove them.

Before Amazon launched the Neutral Evaluation program, there was not a good system—for brands or for sellers—to address patent infringement on the Marketplace. Brands had to submit a claim to Amazon that an accused product was infringing, and identify the patent at issue, how it was infringing, and the ASINs involved. Amazon could reject these claims for various reasons, and with little explanation. In some cases, patent owners or brands abused the system by asserting false claims of patent infringement against sellers. Amazon, hoping to remain uninvolved in the dispute, removed the accused product and made the seller contact the brand directly to resolve it, which could involve litigation.[13]

BOTTOM LINE: At the time of writing, the Neutral Evaluation program is by invitation-only and limited to utility patents, not other types of patents such as design patents or plant patents. Although it expedites the process of obtaining an evaluation and does not require litigation, it does come at a cost and requires legal briefing likely best handled by patent counsel. As the program has not been rolled out beyond beta test-

---

13. Masters, K. (Sept. 30, 2019) *Amazon's New 'Utility Patent Neutral Evaluation' Process Stops Bogus IP Claims*, https://www.forbes.com/sites/kirimasters/2019/09/30/amazons-new-utility-patent-neutral-evaluation-process-stops-bogus-ip-claims/#7323c41f4468 [Accessed January 18, 2020]

ing, we will continue to keep an eye on Amazon's efforts to curtail patent infringement on its Marketplace.

CHAPTER 8

EUROPEAN STRATEGIES

It is not the strongest or the most intelligent who will survive, but those who can best manage change.

—LEON C. MEGGINSON

BEYOND THE UNITED States, Amazon continues to capture an ever-increasing share of eCommerce. Europe is no exception. Indeed, total eCommerce sales in Europe are now over $600 billion annually, exceeding sales in the United States. Amazon has more than 1.1 million active sellers on its marketplaces in Europe, and continues to outpace its competitor retailers in year-over-year growth.[1] This rapid online marketplace expansion brings with it a number of challenges for manufacturers and brands selling products in the European Economic Area (EEA). Chief among them is the fact that online marketplaces have totally upended traditional distribution models. One thing is certain: brands cannot continue to rely on "business as usual" in this new paradigm.

Many brands grappling with these new market dynamics across Europe are confused and mistakenly believe that they have no recourse. There are, however, clear steps brands can take to best respond to the challenges posed by the fast-expanding online marketplace channel in Europe. Brands can best position themselves to respond to these chal-

---

1. (June 11, 2019) *Ecommerce in Europe: €621 billion in 2019,* https://ecommercenews.eu/ecommerce-in-europe-e621-billion-in-2019/; (Nov. 26, 2019), *Amazon has 1.1 million active sellers in Europe,* https://ecommercenews.eu/amazon-has-1-1-million-active-sellers-in-europe/; Davis, D. (Feb. 21, 2019), *European consumers shop more online—and with Amazon,* https://www.digitalcommerce360.com/article/european-ecommerce/ [Accessed January 18, 2020]

lenges and achieve future success by establishing a legally compliant selective distribution system that requires all sellers—including online marketplace sellers—to meet specified criteria and be accountable to the brand. While selective distribution has historically been associated with "luxury" and other sophisticated products, the realities of the eCommerce—in particular, the online marketplace—channel are causing quality brands across numerous categories to consider this strategy. With selective distribution in place, brands can stop unauthorized sellers through business and legal means. By leveraging selective distribution and careful consideration of the features and capabilities of authorized sellers, brands can position themselves for omnichannel health and a continued high-quality brand experience in this increasingly online marketplace-driven European market.

THE FOUNDATION FOR LONG-TERM BRAND SUCCESS IN THE EUROPEAN MARKET

BRANDS THAT ARE grappling with a loss of control, unauthorized sellers, and the damage they cause must ensure that any actions taken to redress these issues comply with European competition law. Under Article 101(1) of the Treaty on the Functioning of the European Union (TFEU), agreements and concerted practices are not allowed if they have the object or effect of preventing, restricting, or distorting competition. However, an exception exists for agreements or practices that improve the production or distribution of goods, or technical or economic progress, allow consumers a fair share of the resulting benefit, and do not impose unnecessary restrictions or create the possibility of eliminating competition.[2]

While this language is quite broad, European authorities have provided guidance on how brands can manage their sellers in a lawful manner. In particular, European courts and regulators have made clear that brands may sell their products through a selective distribution system that meets certain requirements. For many brands, implementing a lawful and

---

2. Consolidated Version of the Treaty on the Functioning of the European Union Art. 101(3), [2008] OJ 115, 09/05/2008, pp. 0088—0089, https://eur-lex.europa.eu/LexUriServ/LexUriServ.do?uri=CELEX:12008E101:EN:HTML [Accessed January 18, 2020]

effective selective distribution system in Europe will be the best way to protect themselves from the harms caused by unauthorized sellers.

Importantly, as discussed further below, when designing selective distribution systems and related reseller criteria, brands must be conscious of the entirely new "ecosystem" at play in the marketplace-driven world of eCommerce. This new ecosystem requires a new way of thinking for brands in terms of the characteristics of high-quality resellers. More specifically, brands must now give careful thought to the qualities sought across three distinct categories of resellers: brick-and-mortar, online, and online marketplace, as each category comes with its own distinct business realities.

Selective Distribution—The Basics

By implementing a lawful selective distribution system, a brand can achieve significant control over where and how its products may be sold in an authorized manner. In a selective distribution system, brands sell only to authorized sellers who satisfy certain stated criteria of a qualitative and/or quantitative nature. These authorized sellers then sell to other authorized sellers within the selective distribution system (that also meet the criteria) or to end users. Authorized sellers may not sell to unauthorized sellers outside the system. Once implemented, selective distribution allows brands to cut off supply to authorized sellers who divert products outside of the system and bring legal claims against unauthorized sellers that may have acquired products but do not satisfy the stated selective distribution criteria.

When implementing selective distribution, brands must give careful thought to choosing appropriate selective distribution criteria. Importantly, brands do not have absolute discretion in setting their criteria. Rather, any criteria that are implemented must satisfy the three *Metro* requirements; that is, they must be: (1) *legitimate* (*i.e.*, justified by the nature of the product or brand in question); (2) *objective* (*i.e.*, applied uniformly to all potential sellers); and (3) *necessary* (*i.e.*, no more restrictive than needed to achieve the legitimate objective).[3]

Although all selective distribution criteria must meet these requirements, brands with a lower market share typically have more discretion in setting their criteria. In particular, the Vertical Block Exemption Regulation (VBER)[4] creates a safe harbor when the market share of both the brand and each authorized seller is under 30%. When VBER applies to a selective distribution system, that system is "exempted"—in other words, it is presumed to be lawful so long as it does not include certain "hardcore" restrictions, discussed below. Importantly, VBER is not a substitute for the *Metro* requirements; selective distribution criteria exempted by VBER must still be legitimate, objective, and necessary. However, when VBER applies, a brand can often avoid having to engage in a detailed competitive analysis.

If a brand's market share is too high to be exempted under VBER (above 30%), it can still implement selective distribution, but should first perform a self-assessment of its desired criteria to ensure they meet the *Metro* requirements. This self-assessment should describe the benefits that selective distribution will have for consumers and the brand's reputation (such as superior quality control, customer service, seller accountability, brand image or prestige, etc.), and the key competitive characteristics of the relevant product and geographic markets (such as market shares, competitors, barriers to entry, etc.). The brand should then be prepared to show that any selective distribution criteria will serve the intended purposes of the selective distribution system, while having minimal effects on competition in the relevant markets.

Under European law, a distinction exists between "qualitative" and "quantitative" selective distribution criteria. Qualitative criteria are those that relate to the quality of the product or brand, and do not directly limit the quantity of sellers. For example, qualitative criteria may include

---

3. European Commission, *Guidelines on Vertical Restraints* [2010] OJ C 130, 19/5/2010, pp. 1-46, ¶ 175, https://ec.europa.eu/competition/antitrust/legislation/guidelines_vertical_en.pdf (citing Case 26/76 Metro I [1977] ECR 1875, paragraphs 20 and 21) [Accessed January 18, 2020]

4. Commission Regulation (EU) No 330/2010 of 20 April 2010 on the application of Article 101(3) of the Treaty on the Functioning of the European Union to categories of vertical agreements and concerted practices, [2010] OJ L 102, 23/4/2010, pp. 1-7, https://eur-lex.europa.eu/eli/reg/2010/330/oj [Accessed January 18, 2020]

requirements that sellers have experience selling the products at issue, employ trained sales personnel, provide certain customer services, or carry a certain range of the brand's products. Quantitative selective distribution criteria are those that directly limit the quantity of sellers, such as limiting the total number of sellers or requiring each seller to have a minimum or maximum amount of sales.

Generally speaking, qualitative criteria are more easily implemented. Quantitative criteria can also be used if the brand's market share is low enough to be exempted under VBER. Brands with market shares in excess of 30% should consider using purely qualitative selective distribution. Example qualitative and quantitative criteria are set forth on the following pages.

Example selective distribution criteria

Given this relevant legal framework and the common problems faced by brands in the eCommerce channel, there are numerous possible selective distribution criteria that would enable prioritization of high-quality resellers across a number of product categories. Of course, each criterion implemented must be legitimate, objective, and necessary in the context of the specific brand and market situation. However, the following categories may be a starting point for brands in developing selective distribution criteria that address the most common problems encountered in the eCommerce age.

- MARKETPLACE CHANNEL CRITERIA (QUALITATIVE) Online marketplace sellers may be required to meet certain criteria intended to address the unique issues brands face in the marketplace channel. For example, sellers may be required to maintain a minimum seller rating or maximum defect rate, provide the brand with access to the seller's marketplace profile and analytics, or opt out of marketplace policies that may imperil product quality such as marketplace inventory commingling and repackaging policies. In some cases, brands may also consider banning sales on particularly problematic marketplaces altogether.

- SELLER ACCOUNTABILITY (QUALITATIVE). Sellers may be required to have a minimum experience or reputation selling the product category, allow the brand to inspect their facilities and records, refrain from using any fulfillment practices that could result in commingling of inventory with that of other resellers, report complaints and other issues to the brand, designate an employee to be in charge of compliance, or periodically certify compliance to the brand.

- CUSTOMER SERVICE (QUALITATIVE). Sellers may be required to conspicuously identify their business name and contact information on any website or storefront, have sufficient knowledge to answer customer questions about the products, or promptly respond to customer inquiries. This type of criterion can address the problems caused by sellers who are nonresponsive to customer problems, which frequently is the case with unauthorized online marketplace sellers.

- PRODUCT DESCRIPTION (QUALITATIVE). Sellers may be required to use only the product descriptions and images approved by the brand, identify any used or repackaged product accordingly and not resell it as new, or clearly identify on every product listing the country the product is intended for, languages the product supports, and any other applicable country-specific requirements. Online marketplace customers frequently complain about ordering one product and receiving another. For instance, they may have ordered a new product but received a repackaged one (which is more likely to be damaged or otherwise of lesser quality), as many marketplaces allow repackaged products to be sold as new. In Europe, customers sometimes face the additional problem of receiving a product intended for use in a different European country, which may not support their local language or be compatible with their country's standards or infrastructure. These criteria help ensure that customers get what they order.

- FULFILLMENT (QUALITATIVE). Sellers may be required to follow shipping and handling requirements when shipping products to a customer, inspect products prior to shipment for issues such as damage, expiration, broken seals, or incorrect weight, or refrain from fulfilling products in a way that could result in inventory commingling. Many customers encounter fulfillment problems when ordering online and, when this occurs, often blame the brand because they cannot tell if the product was mishandled by the seller or the brand. Brands can reduce the risk of mishandling by requiring all sellers to abide by certain fulfillment requirements.

- STORAGE (QUALITATIVE). Sellers may be required to store products under certain temperature and humidity conditions, maintain an appropriate warehouse that the brand can inspect, or discard products that appear visibly damaged, have an otherwise unusual appearance, or are expired. These requirements may be particularly appropriate for ingestible products, as customers buying such products from online sellers frequently receive products that are stale, expired, rotten, rancid, moldy, or damaged by improper storage.

- PRODUCT PACKAGING (QUALITATIVE). Sellers may be prohibited from altering product packaging, repackaging products, or altering products, or may be required to visually inspect products prior to shipment to verify that no such alteration has taken place. When products are repackaged or altered, customers face a higher risk of receiving the wrong product, or a product that is missing parts or other important informational materials.

- MARKETING CONTRIBUTIONS (QUALITATIVE). Sellers may be required to contribute a proportional amount of money or services to the brand's marketing programs, cooperate with such programs, or carry the brand's full product range. These requirements incentivize sellers to promote the entire brand, and discourage free-riding.

- BRAND IMAGE (QUALITATIVE). Sellers may be required to follow the brand's rules regarding appearance and product placement in their store or website, maintain a reputation and image consistent with that promoted by the brand, or follow the brand's rules for the use of its trademarks, product descriptions, images, or other intellectual property. These image requirements are one of the most common reasons for having selective distribution, as brands (particularly quality brands) seek to maintain the perceived value of their products. As many European authorities have recognized, low-quality sellers can hurt a brand's image, so brands attempting to cultivate a high-quality image may consider selective distribution.

- QUANTITATIVE CRITERIA. If the brand has a market share below the 30% threshold and is therefore exempted under VBER, it may also consider quantitative criteria such as limits on the number of sellers or a minimum seller size. By reducing the total number of sellers, these quantitative criteria will allow smaller brands to monitor and manage their sellers with more limited resources.

Avoid all hardcore restrictions

Regardless of market share, every brand must avoid implementation of any "hardcore" restrictions in Europe. As respects eCommerce and the implementation of selective distribution, three categories of hardcore restrictions merit discussion here: (1) resale price maintenance; (2) discrimination against online sellers; and (3) prohibitions on cross-sales within a selective distribution system.

Resale price maintenance

Brands should avoid any pricing-related restrictions in Europe. Any restriction that directly or indirectly constitutes a fixed or minimum sale price is considered a hardcore restriction. Importantly, a restriction need not be contained in a formal or written policy to be deemed unlawful. Recently, the European Commission fined four consumer electronics brands over €111 million for resale price maintenance because those brands pressured, rewarded, or penalized sellers on the issue of pricing, even though the brands did not have formal written pricing policies.[5] Notably, European regulators have determined that MAP policies are

---

5. European Commission (2018) *Antitrust: Commission fines four consumer electronics manufacturers for fixing online resale prices,*https://europa.eu/rapid/press-release_IP-18-4601_en.htm [Accessed January 18, 2020]

impermissible resale price maintenance tactics, so brands should not implement MAP policies in Europe.[6]

Europe's ban on resale price maintenance has implications for online price monitoring as well. Brands routinely employ price monitoring for a variety of legitimate reasons, such as setting wholesale prices or estimating the retail market value of their products. While these types of activities are not unlawful in and of themselves, brands must take steps to ensure that such information is not inadvertently used improperly. Best practices for any brand using online price monitoring include ensuring that all relevant employees are adequately trained on compliance issues, and that internal controls exist and are documented to ensure that the monitoring is used only for legitimate purposes.

Finally, resale price maintenance does not include having a maximum or recommended price, as long as there is no pressure or incentive to follow a minimum or fixed price. Accordingly, a brand can print suggested retail prices on its products or advertising, so long as it does not pressure sellers to comply. As with price monitoring, proper training is the best course of action for ensuring that adequate compliance measures are in place.

Online sales

Brands may not discriminate against online sellers when establishing selective distribution. European authorities treat online sales as an important channel for consumers, and national regulators have fined brands on a number of occasions for banning online sales or putting restrictions on online sales so onerous as to amount to de facto bans. For example, in the recent *Stihl* case, the French competition authority fined a chainsaw manufacturer for requiring all products to be hand-delivered, as the hand-

---

6. Office of Fair Trading (March 27, 2014) Competition Act 1998: Decision of the Office of Fair Trading, CE/9578-12,https://assets.publishing.service.gov.uk/media/5452205 1ed915d1380000007/Pride_Decision_Confidential_Version.pdf [Accessed January 18, 2020]

delivery requirement defeated the convenience of online shopping and thus constituted a de facto online sales ban.[7]

Despite these limitations, however, brands can still require online sellers to follow quality controls and satisfy selective distribution criteria. A brand's selective distribution criteria must simply be "overall equivalent" for online sellers and brick-and-mortar sellers. This requirement does not mean that online and brick-and-mortar criteria must be identical; rather, the two types of criteria must pursue the same objectives and achieve comparable results, with any differences between them justified by the different nature of the online channel.

Cross-sales within selective distribution system

A selective distribution system also must allow cross-sales between its members. In other words, any authorized seller in the selective distribution system must be allowed to purchase products from any other authorized seller in the selective distribution system (regardless of whether those sellers operate at the wholesale or retail level of trade). Furthermore, authorized sellers at the retail level must be free to sell to all end users, although authorized sellers at the wholesale level can be restricted from selling to some or all end users in order to preserve two-step distribution.

OTHER POSSIBLE DISTRIBUTION APPROACHES TO PROTECT AND GROW YOUR BRAND

ALTHOUGH SELECTIVE DISTRIBUTION will often be the best approach for companies seeking to protect brand equity in Europe, other possibilities exist as well. Two other approaches that certain brands can consider are: (1) exclusive distribution; and (2) agency.

---

7. Autorité de la concurrence (2018) *The Autorité de la concurrence fines the manufacturer Stihl 7 million euros for having prevented its authorized distributors from selling its products online*, http://www.autoritedelaconcurrence.fr/user/standard.php?id_rub=684&id_article=3290&lang=en [Accessed January 18, 2020]

Exclusive Distribution

This involves the appointment of a single seller to cover a particular territory or group of customers. As with selective distribution, exclusive distribution is generally exempted under VBER so long as the brand and seller do not exceed the 30% market share threshold and do not use hardcore restrictions. Where the parties' market share exceeds 30%, exclusive distribution must generally be justified by the need to incentivize sellers to invest in the brand.

In an exclusive distribution system, sellers can be prohibited from actively selling (*i.e.*, actively soliciting customers) into other sellers' exclusive markets (whether territory or customer group), but cannot be prohibited from passively selling (*i.e.*, responding to customer orders). Passive selling includes operating a website that is not specifically targeted to another seller's market and fulfilling orders that customers place on that website. One exception to this rule is that, if a seller had to make substantial investments to develop a new market for the brand's products, the brand can restrict passive sales by other sellers into that market for up to two years.

Exclusive distribution may be a particularly effective strategy for brands executing their initial European launch and where having a single seller may be advantageous. These brands could always expand into a broader selective distribution system later as the product market in Europe expands.

Agency

This involves a brand selling its products through a bona fide agent. Agents are not considered to exist independently of the brand, so there can be no unlawful agreement or concerted practice between a brand and its agent for competition law purposes. Therefore, a brand could limit its agents' territory and customers, and even set its agents' prices and other terms of sale, without running afoul of competition laws (although brands with a dominant market position must still take care to avoid unilateral abuse of dominance). Accordingly, brands that want maximum involvement and control in their European distribution might consider selling through bona fide agents.

To qualify as a bona fide agent, an agent must not bear any significant risks regarding the product and market. Thus, an agent cannot have any property rights in the brand's products and would typically be paid by commission. Furthermore, agents cannot be required to contribute to any costs relating to the goods, such as transportation, storage, or marketing (although agents can be required to do the actual transportation, storage, or marketing as long as the costs are reimbursed by the brand). Finally, agents cannot bear any liability risks relating to the goods (such as the risk that the goods will be destroyed or that customers will not pay) unless the agent is itself at fault.

A THREE-STEP PROCESS FOR IMPLEMENTING THE STRATEGY BEST SUITED TO PROTECT AND GROW YOUR BRAND IN THE ECOMMERCE AGE

BRANDS SEEKING TO best meet the challenges of the eCommerce age can engage in the following three-step process to position themselves for long-term success: (1) develop a go-to-market strategy that supports brand equity and business goals; (2) implement the legal and commercial foundation needed to support this strategy; and (3) conduct effective enforcement against unauthorized sellers that disrupt this strategy.

Setting the go-to-market strategy

A brand should first consider how it wants to go to market in Europe. This involves defining what its ideal distribution model would be in light of the rise of eCommerce and online marketplaces. There are several questions that a brand should answer in developing its strategy in today's market, such as:

- WHAT ARE THE MAJOR PAIN POINTS THE BRAND IS FACING? Is the brand unable to meaningfully enforce its quality standards in the current environment, are the brand's image and reputation being degraded, or are sellers refusing to invest in the brand due to the presence of free-riding, low-quality unauthorized sellers?
- WHAT IS THE BRAND'S MARKET SHARE?

- WHAT KIND OF AUTHORIZED SELLERS DOES THE BRAND WANT TO CULTIVATE, INCLUDING ON ONLINE MARKET-PLACES? Does it want only sellers who fit a certain image or only sellers who have experience with certain products or customer segments, and does it want to prioritize sellers who can satisfy its quality controls and are accountable to the brand?
- WHAT ARE THE MAJOR KNOWN OR SUSPECTED SOURCES OF PRODUCTS BEING OBTAINED BY LOW-QUALITY UNAUTHO-RIZED SELLERS?
- WHAT IS THE BRAND'S STRATEGY REGARDING ONLINE MARKETPLACES? On which online marketplaces would the brand like to sell? On Amazon, would it like to sell through a 1P model, a company-owned 3P storefront, or through high-quality 3P sellers?
- WHAT QUALITY CONTROLS ARE APPROPRIATE FOR THE BRAND'S PRODUCTS? What types of issues are consumers complaining about? Do any products require special instructions or handling? Do customers require any post-sale support? Are any products subject to safety or regulatory concerns in any European country?
- HOW DOES THE BRAND WANT TO POSITION ITSELF? Does the brand want to be a luxury brand, a high-quality brand, a mass market premium brand, or a brand that fills some kind of niche?
- WHAT PRODUCT AND GEOGRAPHIC MARKETS DOES THE BRAND COMPETE IN, AND WHAT ARE THE COMPETITIVE CONDITIONS IN THOSE MARKETS? What is the brand's market share, who are the brand's main competitors, and what barriers to entry or other competitive dynamics exist in those markets?
- HOW DOES EUROPE FIT INTO THE BRAND'S GLOBAL STRATEGY? Is the brand positioned the same around the world, or differently in different regions? What distribution and grey market mitigation strategies are the brand following elsewhere?
- WHAT STAKEHOLDERS (BOTH INTERNAL AND AMONG CHANNEL PARTNERS) WILL NEED TO ALIGN ON THE

BRAND'S DISTRIBUTION STRATEGY FOR IT TO BE SUCCESS-
FUL?

With the massive retail revolution well underway, brands need to give careful consideration to these questions notwithstanding how they may have "done things" in the past. Through the process of answering these questions, brands will be empowered to develop the best strategy for their particular circumstances. For example, once the brand has determined the problems its products and customers encounter, the types of sellers and market position it wants, and its applicable market share, the brand will be able to structure its selective distribution criteria to exclude those sellers who are unable to satisfy the criteria and prioritize those that do.

Foundation

With a clear strategy in place, the next step is to implement the necessary legal and commercial foundation in a manner that is both lawful and acceptable to both key internal stakeholders and channel partners. A brand's key foundational components will typically include the following:

- MASTER SELECTIVE DISTRIBUTION MEMORANDUM. The brand should memorialize all of its selective distribution criteria in a single document. This will ensure that there is no confusion about what the brand's requirements are and that the brand will apply its criteria evenly.
- AGREEMENTS OR POLICIES WITH AUTHORIZED SELLERS. These agreements or policies will commit authorized sellers to following the selective distribution criteria, prohibit authorized sellers from selling to unauthorized sellers, and reserve the brand's right to terminate breaching sellers. They can also include commercial terms the brand wishes to have with its authorized sellers.
- INTERNAL SELECTIVE DISTRIBUTION POLICY. The brand should draft an internal policy that its employees can follow, laying out how the selective distribution system is structured and how it will be enforced. Having such a policy will help

the brand enforce its selective distribution system consistently and evenhandedly.

- SELF-ASSESSMENT OPINION. Finally, if a brand is a not exempted under VBER (*i.e.*, its market share exceeds 30%), it should perform a self-assessment, ideally with the assistance of competition counsel, to demonstrate that the selective distribution criteria it uses are fully compliant with the *Metro* requirements and will not have an adverse impact on competition.

Once the foundational documents are in place, the brand will be prepared to roll out its selective distribution system. While each brand's rollout process will depend on its unique circumstances and relationships, several key steps should typically be taken to ensure that it is well-received by customers:

- COVER LETTERS AND TALKING POINTS FOR CHANNEL CUSTOMERS. Clear cover letters and talking points to channel customers will help the brand accurately communicate the goals and requirements of the selective distribution system.
- INTERNAL TRAINING FOR EMPLOYEES (INCLUDING LEGAL COMPLIANCE). The brand should train its employees to ensure they do not inadvertently run afoul of any laws in implementing and enforcing the selective distribution system.
- PROCESS FOR HANDLING APPLICATIONS AND VETTING POTENTIAL SELLERS. Once the brand has established its selective distribution system, potential sellers will apply to join the system, and the brand will review their applications to determine whether they meet the selective distribution criteria. The process for doing so is best settled prior to roll-out.

Unauthorized seller enforcement

Finally, once a brand has aligned on its strategy and implemented the requisite foundation, it should enforce its selective distribution system against unauthorized sellers. This is typically accomplished by leveraging national tortious interference or unfair competition laws. This enforcement discussion presumes that a brand's trademark rights have been exhausted. If exhaustion does not apply, other enforcement options will likely exist. Brands can use the following process for enforcement.

- MONITORING AND IDENTIFICATION. The brand should begin by monitoring online marketplaces for unauthorized sellers and determining which sellers should be prioritized based on the relative amount of brand damage being caused. There are many technological solutions that can automate this process, track relevant data, and generate reports. These technologies can also strengthen a brand's legal claims by gathering evidence of disruption, such as poor reviews tied to particular sellers. Of course, the brand should ensure that any monitoring software is fully compliant with European law.

- BUSINESS ENFORCEMENT. After identifying an unauthorized seller, the brand should remove them by business means if possible. If the seller does not meet the requisite criteria for the channel at issue, the brand can cut off its sources. Business enforcement may resolve the brand's problems without the need for further legal proceedings and will also strengthen a brand's legal claims if legal proceedings are required. In some countries, a brand must show that it actually enforces its selective distribution rules before it can bring a legal claim against an unauthorized seller.

- INVITATION TO APPLY. If the seller is unknown, the brand should send a formal letter informing the seller of the brand's selective distribution rules and inviting the seller to apply to join the selective distribution system if the seller can certify that it meets the applicable criteria. Giving sellers a chance to apply for authorized status is advisable. If the seller is unable or unwilling to comply with the selective distribution criteria, the brand will have the basis needed to justify the seller's exclusion from the system and enforcement against the seller for interfering with the system should it continue to sell.

- CEASE-AND-DESIST LETTERS. If an unauthorized seller is not accepted into the selective distribution system and continues to sell, the brand should send a formal cease-and-desist letter informing the seller of its violation of the brand's selective distribution rules and the brand's legal claims against it. Many sellers will stop selling at this stage as they will want to avoid incurring further legal risk.

- LEGAL ENFORCEMENT. If cease-and-desist letters are ineffective, then the brand will be positioned to pursue escalated legal action against the unauthorized seller. It should determine the best jurisdiction available, together with the litigation processes in that jurisdiction, and govern its legal strategy accordingly.

CHAPTER 9

SELLING UPWARD

A cynic is a man who knows the price of everything and the value of nothing.

—Oscar Wilde

IF THE TRIALS and tribulations discussed in this book sound familiar, your brand, like so many others, likely needs to implement the approaches described herein. To do so, it is important to first internally audit your company and begin to gather your key stakeholders. Only then can you begin to do what we call "selling upward." As described in Chapter 6, evolving into a brand that is equipped for online channels requires a number of strategic decisions, as well as operational changes.

For many long-standing brands, senior management may not yet have fully recognized the rapid rise in importance of online marketplaces and the challenges they create for unprepared brands. These include:

1. BRANDING: Is your brand being properly represented online? Is someone else selling your brand using complete, correct and consistent branding and messaging? Or, instead, has minimal effort been put into representing your brand online, potentially causing customer confusion or a poor consumer experience? Is an unauthorized seller generating poor product reviews on Amazon due to product quality issues? For the millions of dollars your firm may be spending on branding each year, is anyone in your firm paying attention to branding in these online marketplaces?

2. CHANNEL CONFLICT: Is there conflict between your online and brick-and-mortar channels? Are consumers engaging in

showrooming? Are your distributors and retailers complaining about the state of your brand online?

3. SHARE OF VOICE: Are your brand's key competitors already more active on Amazon than you? Are your competitors getting more share of the voice on Amazon than you would expect? Are smaller, less familiar brands winning on organic search results on Amazon?

Whether you want your brand to be available for sale on Amazon or not, if your brand is popular, someone will find a way to sell your products on Amazon. To put it bluntly, if you do not represent your brand on Amazon, someone else will do it for you, and they will do it their way. To confirm whether your brand's products are being sold on Amazon, you can do a very simple product search of your brand on an online marketplace like Amazon to review your products. As part of this search, attempt to gather the following information, all publicly viewable on Amazon:

1. How many of your brand's products are available for sale on Amazon.com today?
2. What is the average number of reviews of your brand's products? What are the average scores of reviews on your brand of products?
3. What level of channel conflict exists between Amazon and your brick-and-mortar channels?
4. What kinds of photographs are being used to represent your brand's products on Amazon? Are they high-quality? Are they the types of photos you want to represent your brand?
5. What monthly sales revenue is being generated from your brand's products on Amazon? What about key competitors' monthly sales revenue?
6. How many of your products are Prime-eligible (available for two-day shipping by Amazon)? Products that are not Prime-eligible are much less likely to be found, or purchased, by Amazon customers.

Tools like Junglescout.com also can help you gauge the relative size of your brand's category on Amazon. They will tell you what volume of your brand is being sold today. In addition, Keepa.com and CamelCamel-Camel.com among others can help you look at historical information of specific product listings, allowing you to see price fluctuations and changes in available inventory.

If your search reveals low-quality or inaccurate product images, incomplete product descriptions, and conflict with content and sellers in your other channels, these are signs that it is time to develop and roll out an effective channel control strategy. As a starting point, we encourage you to circulate a report of your findings to senior leadership and meet with them to address the damage caused to your brand by unauthorized online sales.

If you can get the attention of your senior leadership this way, they next need to consider the following questions:

1. Does your brand have a centralized Product Information Management (PIM) platform with the appropriate assets for organic search and customer conversion purposes on Amazon?
2. What legal controls does your brand have to determine and enforce which resellers will represent your brand in online marketplaces like Amazon?
3. What conversations have occurred between the sales department and the eCommerce department within your brand to minimize the likelihood of the sales team knowingly selling product that goes on to supply diverters participating in online marketplaces like Amazon?

With the involvement of senior leadership, you can begin to develop a channel control strategy. Buy Box Experts and Vorys have found that the most competitive online brands have built a legally compliant online strategy that starts with tight control of distribution in other channels. That requires discipline and policing that most brands traditionally have not required when selling only into retail outlets.

While distribution control discussions are underway, additional attention should be paid to the following areas:

1. *Becoming less dependent on a MAP/MSRP policy*: Most of a brand's Amazon channel distribution problems will be with

unauthorized sellers that are not going to pay any attention to a MAP/MSRP policy anyway. Building and implementing an effective authorized reseller program is a more involved effort than putting together a MAP/MSRP policy.

2. *Short-term sales impact*: Should a brand decide to restrict which distributors and resellers can participate in online channels like Amazon, it is reasonable to expect that, in the short term, the brand's sales to wholesale channels may drop. This is because sellers forbidden from selling on Amazon will no longer place purchase orders to fatten up their online inventory for the Amazon channel, and wholesale inventory gets flushed out into retail channels. Depending on whether the brand chooses to buy back inventory from distributors and retailers, it may take three to nine months to get back to consistent wholesale volumes.

3. *Short-term challenges in obtaining channel alignment and identifying appropriate long-term partners by channel*: If you determine that certain distributors and resellers or retailers can no longer sell on Amazon, the brand's leaders will have to communicate effectively with them, reassuring them that better control over online and brick-and-mortar sales channels is best in the long-term for the brand and the sellers.

4. *Longer-term pricing alignment*: It can take six to twelve months for distribution control to be implemented, allowing a brand to stabilize advertised prices on Amazon and align them with advertised retail pricing in brick-and-mortar channels. But it is critical to get to this point so that end customers are incentivized to purchase through authorized channels and the brand can both protect and rebuild its brand equity.

5. *Longer-term branding impact*: Depending on how quickly a brand can develop the necessary digital assets to optimize its listings on Amazon, it may take six months or more to create a high-quality set of online product listings, consistent in content and messaging with the brand's offline marketing and product content.

6. *Longer-term ability to collect end-consumer data and to gauge changing end-consumer preferences*: Eventually, a brand may

choose to become a B2C operation on Amazon, giving it access to end-user data, and a retail environment where it can experiment with new product variations or new product bundles. This opportunity to collect data and experiment is rare for most brands today, but it is becoming easier to leverage for brands that embrace the opportunities that the Amazon Marketplace presents.

When a brand lacks the policies and procedures to control sales in online marketplaces in accordance with applicable laws, the repercussions across the brand's overall business can be negative and long-term. An eCommerce or other executive's efforts to get the attention of senior management is critical, and should be data-driven to show the potentially disastrous impact on the brand. As eCommerce grows and the marketplaces tighten their grip on retail market share, brand executives must take immediate steps, using the approaches discussed throughout this book, to assert control over their online sales. Inaction is not a viable strategy, as the market forces at play will inevitably cause significant damage to brand image and value if left unaddressed. Brand executives will be well on their way to controlling their brands, both online and offline, if they proactively manage consistent branding and carefully monitor and police distribution of their products across all channels.

SECTION 4

APPENDIX

GLOSSARY

AMAZON FLYWHEEL
The visualization of the strategy Amazon has developed to drive the growth of its Marketplace. See Chapter 2, Figure 1.

AMAZON MARKETPLACE
The eCommerce platform owned and operated by Amazon that enables third-party sellers to sell new or used products on a fixed-price online marketplace alongside Amazon's regular offerings. At the time of writing, the marketplace contains over 3 million sellers and 500 million product listings available for sale.

ASIN / AMAZON STANDARD IDENTIFICATION NUMBER
A 10-character alphanumeric unique identifier assigned by Amazon and its partners for product identification within the Amazon organization. Typically structured as B00XXXXXXX (B00 followed by an alphanumeric string, this is also known as the "B00" number for a product).

AUTHORIZED SELLER
The manufacturer or trademark owner may designate which retailers/ resellers it wants to offer its products to customers in specific sales channels. These retailers and resellers are said to be authorized by the brand to sell those products. See also UNAUTHORIZED SELLER. A retailer may be authorized to sell in certain channels, but not in others.

BRAND GATING
A process by which Amazon may, upon agreement with the brand, restrict other sellers' access to sell the brand's products. This program

is not meant to be used by brands to remove unauthorized sellers from Amazon.

Branding Governance

A brand company's efforts to ensure that all the online content that describes the brand and its products is used in a manner consistent with all the other channels in which the brand company shares messaging with consumers.

Branded Product

A generic item in which investments have been made to secure the consistent delivery of unique features and benefits to customers.

Brand Registry

A program developed by Amazon to help brands that have a registered trademark to provide authoritative content to the Amazon catalog.

Channel Conflict

Occurs when a brand's products are being sold by unauthorized sellers and in unauthorized channels, causing repercussions for the brand's equity and its authorized sellers.

Catalog Optimization

A brand company's efforts to ensure that the content on listings of its products is correct and complete. This also involves resolving catalog issues caused by other sellers' improper and unauthorized data submissions on product listings.

Channel Governance

A brand company's efforts to control which companies can sell the brand online, and how they may do so. Strong channel governance helps a brand avoid Channel Conflict (see above).

Commingling

Products of one seller being mixed in fulfillment centers with products of other sellers.

COUNTERFEIT

A fraudulent imitation of a product, meant to fool consumers into believing it is the authentic product.

DISPLAY NAME

The DBA name (see below) used by third-party sellers on Amazon which may differ from their legal name. The use of display names by third-party sellers on Amazon has made it easier for unauthorized sellers to hide their true identity from brands that struggle to figure out the identity of the sellers.

DBA (DOING BUSINESS AS)

A company is said to be "doing business as" when the name under which they operate differs from their legal, registered name.

DISTRIBUTOR

A type of authorized seller within a brand's distribution strategy. Typically, distributors may sell products to retailers, who may then sell to end users.

END USER

The final consumer of a product. End users will not resell products.

EXCLUSIVE DISTRIBUTION

A method of selling products that occurs when a brand appoints a single seller to cover a particular territory or group of customers. In the European Economic Area, such a system must follow certain legal requirements.

FBA (FULFILLMENT BY AMAZON)

A fulfillment service offered by Amazon to third-party sellers where the seller stores its products in Amazon's fulfillment centers, and Amazon picks, packs and ships these products. If a third-party seller puts its products into the FBA program, those products become PRIME-ELIGIBLE (see below). The use of the FBA program can result in COMMINGLING (see above).

FIRST-PARTY (1P)

For brands (or the brands' distributors) that wholesale product directly to Amazon (where Amazon becomes the seller of record on the Amazon Marketplace), the relationship between the brand and Amazon is called a FIRST-PARTY (1P) relationship. See also VENDOR CENTRAL and VENDOR MANAGER.

FIRST SALE DOCTRINE

A doctrine which states that it is generally legal, with some exceptions, for an individual to resell a trademarked item, even if the resale is without the trademark owner's consent. This doctrine governs how an unauthorized seller can be liable for trademark infringement for selling a brand's trademarked products.

GREY MARKETS (SEE ALSO PRODUCT DIVERSION)

Markets in which products are sold outside authorized manufacturer channels. Often the original manufacturer or trademark holder will identify companies that it wants to be the approved (a.k.a. authorized) retailer/reseller of its products. Sometimes individuals are able to source the product indirectly, getting product that has been *diverted*, meaning without permission of the manufacturer. These individuals may resell the inventory that they have sourced, often at prices that do not align with pricing policies that the brand or manufacturer has implemented.

KEY STAKEHOLDERS

The internal leaders within a brand company involved in eCommerce, sales, and legal functions, as well as any other critical executive. A crucial step to achieving control of unauthorized sales is attaining internal alignment among a brand's key stakeholders.

MANUFACTURER SUGGESTED RETAIL PRICE (MSRP)

The price at which a manufacturer recommends that the retailer sells the product.

MARKETPLACE FLYWHEEL™
A model developed by Buy Box Experts to show how a comprehensive brand governance strategy requires multiple, interconnected activities. See Chapter 4, Figure 2.

MATERIAL DIFFERENCE EXCEPTION
An exception to the FIRST SALE DOCTRINE a brand can rely on to assert trademark infringement if the products sold by unauthorized sellers are 'materially different' from the company's authorized products.

MIDNIGHT RUN PRODUCT
See THIRD-SHIFT PRODUCT.

MINIMUM ADVERTISED PRICE (MAP)
The minimum amount at which a reseller should advertise pursuant to the terms of a MAP policy with a brand. While resellers under the policy are free to advertise and sell at any price, it is a violation of the policy to advertise a product under the MAP policy at a price lower than the MAP. Important, this policy is not an agreement between the brand and the reseller.

PRIME-ELIGIBLE
Amazon operates the Prime program, whereby consumers pay to receive unlimited free shipping on approximately 100 million items sold by Amazon and third-party sellers' products that are in the FBA program.

PRODUCT DIVERSION
The practice of retailers or distributors selling product outside the channels authorized by the brand.

PROJECT ZERO
A program developed by Amazon to help alleviate the presence of counterfeit product on the Amazon Marketplace.

QUALITY CONTROL EXCEPTION

An exception to the FIRST SALE DOCTRINE that a brand can rely on to assert trademark infringement if an unauthorized seller is reselling trademarked products that are outside of the trademark owner's quality control standards and other factors are met.

REVERSE DISTRIBUTOR

A distributor which purchases returned product in bulk, often cleans and repackages it, then resells it.

SELLER CENTRAL

The Amazon portal in which a seller can see the products it is listing, how much inventory it is making available, what orders it has received, how much revenue it has generated and what payments it has received from Amazon, etc.

SELECTIVE DISTRIBUTION

A distribution system by which brands may sell products in the European Economic Area. This system must meet certain requirements under European law, including that it must be legitimate, objective, and necessary.

SHADOW INVENTORY

Inventory that is held by distributors and retailers, still unsold to consumers, and in quantities unknown to the brand.

SKU (STOCK KEEPING UNIT)

A number assigned to a product to identify the price, product options and manufacturer. The SKU is used to track inventory in a retail store.

TEST BUY

The purchase of a product by a company to verify the authenticity of the product. A representative from a brand sold on Amazon might develop a test-buy process, whereby she buys the brand's products from third-party sellers offering the products on Amazon. Upon receipt of the purchases, the brand representative can check the units of the products, and verify if the items are authentic, or examine serial numbers on the product to understand the provenance of the item (thereby establishing a potential source of product being diverted to an unauthorized seller by a known distributor or retailer that handles the brand's products).

THIRD-PARTY/ 3P
The Amazon Marketplace is set up to enable practically anyone to list and sell products. Should a retailer or individual choose to list products on Amazon, they would need to create a THIRD-PARTY (3P) seller account, where they would interface with Amazon through the SELLER CENTRAL portal.

THIRD-SHIFT PRODUCT
Otherwise authentic product manufactured outside of the production times dictated by the brand. It can be a common source of diverted product.

TRANSPARENCY PROGRAM
An item-level authentication service that helps companies to protect their brands and customers from counterfeit products. By applying a customized sticker to each unit, the brand is able to restrict sales on Amazon to only units that contain this Transparency sticker. This program is not meant to be used by brands to remove unauthorized sellers from Amazon.

UNAUTHORIZED SELLER
See also AUTHORIZED SELLER. Should a retailer or reseller be able to find units of product to sell, and then sell them without the permission of the manufacturer or trademark owner, they would be viewed as unauthorized sellers—basically, selling the brand's products without permission. A seller may be authorized to sell in certain channels, but not in others.

UPC (UNIVERSAL PRODUCT CODE)
A barcode symbology that is widely used for tracking trade items in stores. The UPC barcode is printed onto physical products for the

purpose of scanning by retailers to identify the products purchased by consumers.

Amazon's catalog is based on each ASIN having a unique UPC. In theory, a UPC is supposed to appear only once in the Amazon catalog, but there are ways to circumvent that, creating catalog listing issues for Amazon and THIRD-PARTY SELLERS. GS1, an international supply-chain standards organization, develops and maintains global standards for UPCs.

UTILITY PATENT NEUTRAL EVALUATION PROCEDURE

A program launched by Amazon in 2019 to allow brands that own utility patents in their products to attempt to enforce those patents against unauthorized sellers of products on the Amazon Marketplace that allegedly infringe on the patents.

VENDOR CENTRAL

The interface used by brands with a FIRST-PARTY (1P) relationship with Amazon to track inventory levels, Amazon purchase orders and financial inventory.

VENDOR MANAGER

The Amazon representative working in a FIRST-PARTY (1P) relationship with a brand to help them sell their product on VENDOR CENTRAL.

To learn more about GROWING YOUR BRAND, contact:

James Thomson
james@buyboxexperts.com
385-455-4982
buyboxexperts.com

To learn more about CONTROLLING YOUR BRAND, contact:

Whitney Gibson
wcgibson@vorys.com
855-381-6475
vorysecontrol.com

Made in the USA
Columbia, SC
08 March 2020